Cast of Thousands

ANITA
Cast of Thousands
LOOS

Grosset & Dunlap
Publishers · New York
A Filmways Company

For Leo Lerman,
the most civilized of all New Yorkers

Foreword

Last year Bob Markel came to me and said, in effect, "When you were born, you clutched in your little fist a front-row ticket to the great spectacle of the Twentieth Century. I'd like you to supply a record of what you saw for Grosset & Dunlap."

It was a tall order, and I could never have filled it without a great deal of help.

But Bob worked out a contract with my agent and friend, Ray Corsini; and with Bob as our inspiration, the project got under way. First Bob placed the design of the book in the expert hands of Irwin Glusker whose studio is in Carnegie Hall across from where I live, so that Irwin could keep a watchful eye on me. His chief art director, Eloise Vega, took charge of problems as intricate as a Chinese puzzle; and, at the start, she had sizeable help from Victoria Romaine. Assisting with photographic research was Lester Glassner, that high priest of movie buffs, who contributed pictures from his own archives and even supplied long-forgotten facts about myself.

Bob's assistant editor, Diana Price, helped bridge my many lapses, and further editorial guidance was supplied by Jim Neyland who is as companionable as he is expert. They all worked with such interest and enthusiasm that my journey into the past became a romp.

But now that the book is in print, I realize that many characters who should have been included have been left out through sheer force of numbers. So a reader had best romp through it as we did and allow any chips I've overlooked to fall where they may.

Not being a gloomy thinker, I am inclined to see humor in many of the dark doings of this particular point in time—as a defense for which I can only quote the chosen theme of this humble opus: it is lighter than you think.

Contents

1

ORIGINS

Child actors at the turn of the century were as larcenous as they are today. But in a San Francisco production of *Quo Vadis?* my sister Gladys (LEFT) seemed to take show business in stride. My expression, however, reveals that I considered acting a low form of endeavor.

When the female nature reaches its peak of satisfaction it begins to tremble. And I, at an impressionable age, entered a world of females who, almost en masse, trembled over Clark Gable. But even among us girls who met Clark daily at the studio, there were dissidents. I was one, and there was Paulette Goddard who had once confessed to me, "Nothing makes me tremble like diamonds" (thereby providing an inspiration I was later to use in a book).

The motives behind this *tremblement de coeur* are much too complicated to understand; I won't even try to explain why it was that any confrontation, however formal, with a man of brains, sent me into a fair fit of trembling; pushed me into experiences that have never yet failed to transpire.

As far as can be traced, our family was a typically American hodge-podge of misfits, tossed together in a pioneer world that wasn't cramped by competition. But, along with the razzle-dazzle supplied by its off-beat characters, there were certain elements of respectability.

During the mid-1850s in Vermont, my Grandpa George Smith posed with his bride for their wedding picture. Grandma had belonged to a family of Shakers, by name Fairbrother, but she had mysteriously been christened Cleopatra, which may have been an early form of E.S.P. Because Cleopatra Fairbrother emulated her wayward namesake as best she could in word, thought, and deed.

From what I know of Shakers, they took their name from a sort of shaking ritual by which they celebrated their religion. They shook singly and only in company with their own sex. Furthermore, they foreswore cohabitation, refused to procreate, and filled their ranks by proselytizing. Apparently their life-style wasn't sufficiently fascinating to keep the sect alive beyond the early days of the colonies.

The Shakers banded together into communities with the women living alone and the men likewise, and never the twain would meet. Since there is no recorded Shaker village in Vermont, although there were in Maine and New Hampshire, I suspect the Fairbrothers followed their religion rather loosely: living on their own farm and doing as they chose. But the family showed a certain tendency toward hedonism, in the fact that Cleopatra possessed a piano. At any rate, the ecstasy she was supposed to express by shaking was phony, but the larceny behind it was genuine and it may well have passed on to me as an inheritance.

George Smith had been a definite catch for any Shaker farm girl. He had belonged to a prosperous family in rural England but in '49, just after gold was discovered in California, he set sail for New York and intended, on reaching port, to join the gold rush to California.

On reaching the New World, George replenished his finances by a stretch of farm work in the Midwest. After which,

My Grandpa was descended from "yeoman stock," as they call it in Britain. This might smack of Robin Hood and seem rather romantic. It wasn't. It merely indicated that Grandpa came from middle-class farm people and bore the prosaic name of George Smith. But in 1851, George Smith migrated to the New World, and when he married a girl called Cleopatra Fairbrother, he rescued my genes from any danger of normality.

with money in his pocket, he spurned the lowly covered wagon and bought passage to San Francisco on a vessel that sailed around the Horn. The voyage took four long months; but in little more than that time, George forged into the Klamath Mountains of Northern California and discovered a mine that turned out gold dust by the panful.

Ultimately George found life in his mining cabin to be crude; he began to dream of returning to the decorous East, to find a little wife, settle down on a pleasant farm, and raise a family.

So, when rich enough to retire, George leased his mine to a British syndicate and set sail from San Francisco on the first lap of his quest. Now George, who had craved for a bride who was a virgin, should really have stood at home and taken a chance with some trollop in a mining camp. For, while looking over some farmland in Vermont, he met the Fairbrother family and fell for Cleopatra. She seemed to fill George's requirement of virginity; and, for diversion, she could also play the piano. But, one thing George failed to discern, was that his bride had an inner itch for adventure. She wanted to see California.

Goaded by Cleopatra, George consented to take her on a sightseeing trip to the Wild West. But Cleopatra, in order to prevent a return to the rock ribs of Vermont, began to assemble all their belongings for a strictly one-way passage. And she made George buy a grand piano, which had to be dismantled for shipping. By that time, George must have realized he'd been misled; the full extent to which was revealed when his bride disclosed she was taking her young piano-tuner along as well. When questioned about that added starter, Cleopatra must have pouted with as much seduction as a blonde. At any rate, she needled George into giving in, at which moment he became stuck for life.

But Cleopatra was to pay dearly for her wealthy marriage; for when they reached the camp in the Salmon Mountains, her dress was frozen to the horse's saddle, and she had to be chopped loose with a hatchet before Grandpa could carry her across the cabin threshold.

With this risky beginning my heritage, such as I know it, had its start.

With the demise of her consumptive piano-tuner, Cleopatra found that life in the Wild West was grubby and lacking in romance. She soon got her fill of the denizens of the mining camp and urged George to descend from their cabin home and settle in the Valley below. There, George staked out eighty-thousand acres and, as a sideline, started to grow wheat. He also built a home for Cleopatra near Etna, which still exists today much in its original condition.

The main house, of Georgian

The picturesque rail fences of early
California that enclosed Grandpa's
farm were to become a deadly symbol
of confinement to his restless bride.

Long after I was writing western movies
that were filmed on the backlots of
Hollywood, the cameras could have
moved northward and found more
authentic settings in the town of Etna
where I had been born. In those
days, there was more gold in those
hills than in the golden curls of
Mary Pickford.

4

architecture and painted white, is surrounded by stables, barns for farm machinery, a carriage house, a smokehouse for the curing of hams, a milk house, and seen to the far left in the picture, a building where large blocks were cut from ice floes during midwinter and preserved in sawdust. That ice house and the milk house collaborated with an ice-cream freezer to produce a tasty dish all through the heat of summer.

Not visible in this picture is a spring of water, which even in July chilled one's very teeth. Folks go out of their way even today to drink from its rusty tin ladle. And it has always been a rendezvous for tramps.

When we children vacationed at Grandpa Smith's, we were admonished to stay away from the spring when there were tramps around. My obedient brother, Clifford, would always obey, as did docile Gladys. But my love for outlaws began in infancy; as a toddler, I disregarded the warning. I was fascinated by tales they told of places as distant as Eureka, across the mountains, and Red Bluff, in the heart of the Sacramento Valley.

There was one tramp who out-glamored every stranger I had met, up to the age of six. He was romantic, dark, a foreigner, and speaking in fascinating accents, he told me of a place called . . . Paris!

As I listened, a *tremblement de coeur* swept over me that was only to be explained later.

In 1976, most other thoroughfares of California are roaring with traffic, gleaming with neon and darting with Cadillacs, but not the main street of the town of Etna. Etna today looks as primitive as when I first toddled down its wooden sidewalk at the age of four. The placer mines of Salmon Mountain have long since been washed away; and, although the soil of the adjoining valley is excellent, crops can be grown for only half the year. And who needs a California where the sunshine vanishes during winter?

Every family produces a sainted mother, and Minnie Smith was mine. However, reared in that remote valley, even she developed signs of wanderlust. But George Smith managed to keep Minnie's frustrations under control by sending her to Mills Seminary for Young Ladies of Quality. It was near enough to San Francisco for shopping trips and the finery that that city imported directly from Paris, by-passing New York, which snobbish San Franciscans considered merely second choice.

But even when dressed in the latest fashion, Minnie still had to spend her long summer vacations in Scott Valley, beset by lethargy.

But Whoop-de-doo! With the entrance of R. Beers Loos on the scene, Minnie's lethargy took a sharp turn for the better. Every family has its Lothario; he was ours—and was he a lollypop!

5

With her well-to-do background, my mother Minnie was able to go to San Francisco for fashions that, even in those pioneer days, came straight from Paris.

G. D. MORSE.

To describe my Daddy, R. Beers Loos, I must go back to his French heritage for a suitable expression. It is "Oo-la-la."

Louis Heller, *photographer,*

FORT JONES,
SISKIYOU CO., CAL.

The Loos family was of French origin; the name of its female branch being Marlatte. R. Beers' forebears possibly came to the Midwest with the French contingent of Father Marquette; most likely they were mixed up in the French and Indian Wars.

At the age of nineteen, R. Beers Loos had lived in Newcomerstown, Ohio, holding down a job as typesetter on the local newspaper. While setting type, R. Beers had also improvised the local society column, which he sprinkled with jokes. He might thus report on some family celebration: "On Sunday, Grandma Hinkle had a birthday party. The cake would have had to be bigger than Ohio to hold all its candles, but there was plenty of Grade-A snuff for one and all."

One fateful day, word reached R. Beers from a friend who had migrated to the West that there was a scarcity of newsprint in Northern California. R. Beers immediately decided to investigate. An only son, he deserted his widowed mother and took off. And while investigating pioneer territory, R. Beers became overnight a sex symbol—witty to the point of being outrageous, and with that type of urbane good looks that foretells early baldness. Minnie was only one of many girls who fell for R. Beers, and their meeting had all the impact of a California earthquake. The fact that Minnie would be an heiress someday made her tempting bait for that young cavalier from the Midwest.

R. Beers chose to start a newspaper in the town of Sisson, which was two days by stagecoach from where Minnie lived. He then sent East for a hand-press and an outlay of type. While awaiting its arrival, R. Beers started to woo Minnie.

Meanwhile, George Smith, with an eye to exposing Minnie to some reputable males, removed her from Mills Seminary—and the proximity of R. Beers Loos—and sent her East to the co-educational University of Delaware. But if he had hoped to get Minnie away from R. Beers, he had hoped in vain. Although she had plenty of beaus in the East, the image of the charmer she'd left behind never faded; and at length, in a solo elopement from college, Minnie rushed back to the busy charisma of R. Beers Loos, and the trials and tribulations that would last as long as she lived. At any rate, she could console herself, it was never to be humdrum.

In the tedium of Scott Valley, the willful Cleopatra had no other choice than to supply George Smith with a family. Much against her better judgment, she gave him six assorted sexes and temperaments. Two of them died in infancy and two others, Fred and Mae, were too dull for anything more than mere mention here. But the two who remained are worthy of note; a blonde beauty named Nina would carry on with Cleopatra's spirit. And contrary-wise, there was my docile mother Minnie.

To a certain extent, R. Beers went along with Minnie's love for hearth and home, if for no other reason than they kept her busy and left him free to meander. The simple young mother's craving for family ties was rewarded by three children. The eldest was my brother Clifford, who throughout his lifetime carried on in the sterling manner of his Mama. He was her greatest comfort because the two of them were so alike. The youngest of the lot was my sister Gladys, who was pretty and blonde and very average.

But the middle child was me. And I so took after my unpredictable father, that it separated us from the others. We were great companions, but a mystery to the remainder of the family and therefore rather suspect.

Minnie loved us all, but she no more understood me than she understood R. Beers. In his case, she had fallen in love with the unpredictable, but an unpredictable child is different from an unpredictable husband. I was disturbing; I posed problems she couldn't solve. We were never close. I was one of those kiddies who provides entertainment for anyone but a mother.

At the age of two, I burst into a front-page spread of the *Sisson Mascot* when R. Beers put me to work advertising his newspaper. I adored him, in much the way a lady of the sidewalks adores the man who procures jobs for her.

But Mother, blind to the fact that she'd given birth to a dyed-in-the-wool cynic, used to call me "Honeybunch," at which I used to squirm.

Pop was indefatigable in finding jobs for his womenfolk. When we moved up the cultural ladder into San Francisco, Pop ultimately put Gladys and me into the theater.

Child actresses at the turn of the century were just as larcenous as they are today and my quizzical expression when only ten shows a trace of that tough syndrome. My sister Gladys was eight, and we were playing Christian martyrs in a stock company production of *Quo Vadis?* in San Francisco. Gladys, who was blonde and amiable, could take acting in stride; but I, as a brunette, didn't disguise that I considered show business a dull way of life.

I was eight when I played Lord Fauntleroy, but I balked at conformity even then and refused to wear the traditional black velvet suit with its effeminate lace collar. I demanded—and got—an outfit in masculine navy blue.

An early form of publicity was dreamed up as a lobby display for that production of *Quo Vadis?* with the Alcazar Stock Company.

That scene in the Coliseum where we Christian martyrs were being thrown to a wild beast was dubbed in, done by trick photography. I think the lion came from a fur shop where it was used as an advertising gimmick. But because *Quo Vadis?* was a smash hit, the Alcazar advertising staff must have known what

This marked the literary beginning of a child who, born and bred in the Wild West, would in due time grow up to see herself described by a Boston columnist as "catnip for Harvard professors."

In a publicity campaign for *Quo Vadis?* my sister and I were featured as a snack for a man-eating lion. But it is all too apparent that he had already been stuffed with sawdust.

they were doing.

My brother Clifford turned out to be the only solid citizen in the family, except for Mother, of course. He was handsome enough to be a leading man; but, too great a snob to go into show business, he chose to be a doctor.

Together with Dr. Cabot Lodge of Boston, he would later invent that system of group medicine that, under the name of Blue Cross, is now in use throughout the U.S.A.

By the time I was eight, Gladys was six, and she was as tall as I. Strangers used to take us for twins. But twins who were blonde and brunette were such a novelty that when we walked down the street we were looked at, causing Mother to succumb to her only moments of exhibitionism.

Then a disaster struck the family. Gladys, taken overnight by peritonitis, died

My brother Clifford is the prize of our family. He grew up to become an eminent physician and was ultimately a pioneer in the modern system of group medicine. When Clifford died, he left fourteen clinics in Southern California.

My sister was everything that I was not. She was blonde, uncritical, and happy-go-lucky. Had she lived, I doubt she would have left any mark on either show-biz or literary effort. She was far too normal.

before any of us could be prepared for the bitter shock. After that, one of Mother's first comments was to say to me, "People won't notice us anymore, Honeybunch. Now we're like everybody else!" But the fact that R. Beers and I were *not* like everybody else would never assuage my poor Mother's permanent state of bewilderment.

Every family has its naughty aunt. The novelist Graham Greene capitalized on his, and his book *Travels with my Aunt* became a best seller.

Our ribald Auntie was Nina Smith, heir to the passions of Cleopatra. While yet a teenager, she had formed nefarious connections with two lusty farmers in Scott Valley. Both scandals were irreparable, for the young men were married and had offspring. Grandpa George, rather than risk a third scandal, bundled her off to a school in San Francisco.

Nina never reached there; no sooner had the train pulled out of the station than she picked up a fascinating stranger. When the two reached Sacramento, her pick-up, whose name was Horace, whisked Nina off the train and made an honest woman out of her in the City Hall.

While I was yet a child, my uncle-by-marriage-to-Nina became the second love-of-my-life after R. Beers; but Horace Robinson's behavior eclipsed even that of my flashy Pop. In San Francisco, Horace floated millions of dollars worth of bogus Marconi Wireless stock. After which he transferred his operations to New York and London. (A book was recently published about those deals.) Having milked the name of Marconi dry, Horace dreamed up a project that involved plans to build a railroad across the Siberian wastes. Later, the Trans-Siberian Railroad was achieved by more legitimate promoters.

Horace died suddenly, stricken by the wear and tear of flimflam on the muscles of the human heart.

Nina, as the bride of an international con man, traveled far and wide; to New York, London, Paris, and points between. Her dresses were by Paquin in a day when few American girls had even heard of him. But Nina's gin rickeys were by Gordon, and Gordon did her in. She died an alcoholic, as naughty aunts are prone to do. But before Nina took off, she had taught me to look to Paris for my fashions.

As was inevitable, Sisson got too small for R. Beers. The quips with which he threaded his news coverage began to be quoted throughout the West. R. Beers became a rival of the nationally known humorist, Bill Nye. The wit of R. Beers finally reached the San Francisco newspapers, and that city beckoned. My Pop was not one to disregard the sinful magic of its summons.

Pop unloaded the *Sisson Mascot*, which, without his *élan,* soon disappeared. Also, since that time, the

My Auntie Nina came to be an
outstanding clotheshorse. She is here
gazing across some furbelows designed
for her in Paris by Patou. My Uncle-
by-marriage-to-Nina stamped my
young character with a mark I was
never to outgrow. As an international
con man, Horace Robinson's
operations extended from New York
to Rome to Moscow and points as far
west as San Francisco, and there
his path crossed mine. Sensing my

adoration, Horace became fond of me;
and, when I was a child of ten, he
bought me a diamond ring from the
elegant firm of Shreves. In return, he
requested a childish kiss. I refused.
I was frightened of so emotional an
experience. Better to play safe and not
disrupt my peace.

Thank you, Uncle Horace, for being
responsible for my self-restraint.
Or rather should I say, curse you, Uncle
Horace, for my unfulfillment as a female.

town itself has disappeared from maps, having been renamed "Mount Shasta" after the snow-capped mountain that rises above it. The mountain still remains, as far as I know.

San Francisco! Now I was on romantic soil. It was there I had my first contact with a man of real stature; a drinking companion of my Pop's, Jack London. Even as a child I realized that he was special. Pop's wisecracks made me laugh a lot; but Mr. London was a poet, especially when he was tight.

Another friend who frequented our house on Bush Street was a dark, handsome, curly-headed boy who worked in a locksmith's shop. But he was stage-struck, and Pop used his influence to get him a job on the Orpheum Circuit in a sort of newfangled magic act. His name was Harry Houdini, and—little as I held actors in esteem—Harry's quick wit and gift of the gab broke down my resistance.

Other important men were crowding into my life; I came in contact with one of the great geniuses of the theater world, although at the age of seven I scarcely appreciated my luck. This came about because a famous New York star named Blanche Bates had married a San Francisco journalist, and she wanted to impress her bridegroom by playing Nora in the first production of *A Doll's House* ever to be done in America. I was given a role in that production.

My uninspired acting could never have

been improved, but I later had the advantage of being directed by the great New York impresario, David Belasco, whose brother Walter ran the Alcazar Stock Company. Walter had staged a play entitled *Mayflower*, which David had written, and he had brought his brother from New York to direct it.

Careening about in San Francisco, Pop got rid of Mama's money at a fast clip. We then moved south, with Pop taking on such glamorous job carnival companies. By that time, I had outstripped him in financial stability. For I had entered into the most exciting new form of show biz ever to bedazzle the eyes of mankind.

A first-grade class at the Denman
Grammar School on Bush Street
reveals a future authoress in the second
row, third from right.

This two-family structure on Union
Street in San Francisco, was the ideal
background for my childhood
fantasies. It still exists, thanks to the
spirit of San Francisco, which protects
those old wooden facades.

2

THE SILENT YEARS

D.W. Griffith had imported Constance Collier from England to play Lady Macbeth in the silent film version of Shakespeare's play. Here she is flanked by Bessie Love as Lady Macduff. Below, hovering over the dog is Pauline Stark, one of the young beauties whom Griffith was grooming for stardom. Watching from the sidelines is D.W. himself. And when that silent picture reached the screen, one of its credits read, "Subtitles by William Shakespeare and Anita Loos."

My first connection with the movies had come when I was acting in a stock company at San Diego, again playing Lord Fauntleroy, though this time forced by a stubborn management to wear that prissy black velvet suit. One night, bored with my job, I ventured down to the dark stage to watch a short movie that was being run between the acts. I could see it from the reverse side of the screen with the light of the projector casting a bright splotch in the middle.

Realizing that every film must require a plot, I decided to try my hand at writing one. I worked it out the next morning and arrived early at rehearsal in order to climb up into the projection booth and search a film can for an address where I might send my story.

The address I found was "The American Biograph Company, 11 East 14th Street, New York City."

I sent my manuscript there, having signed it A. Loos, which I thought would make me appear to be a man and a more seasoned author. Not more than two weeks went by before I received a long envelope with "American Biograph Company" impressively engraved on the corner. With hands shaking, I tore the envelope apart and removed this letter:

"Mr. A. Loos,
Dear Sir, We have accepted your scenario entitled "The New York Hat." We enclose an assignment which kindly sign and have witnessed by two persons

and then return. On receipt of signed assignment we shall send you our check for $25.00 in payment.

Yours very truly,
Thomas A. Dougherty"

Although unaware of the fact, I had entered the movies at the very top; Dougherty was scenario editor for D.W. Griffith.

There may have been a touch of atavism in my first movie-script, *The New York Hat.* I had placed it in a small Vermont town like the one from which Cleopatra Fairbrother had once fled to escape the boredom of life in New England. And its motivation concerned the heroine's longing for smart millinery, which could only have been inspired by my chic Aunt Nina.

The plot concerned a sadistic miser whose wife and daughter were long-suffering victims of his pinchpenny way of life. In the opening scene, the mother, on her deathbed, was being visited by a handsome young clergyman (Lionel Barrymore). The dying woman had sent for her clergyman in order to hand him a bulky envelope; immediately after which she breathed her last. The preacher found the envelope to contain a sum of money that the poor woman had saved over many years, most of it in pennies held out from the pittances her husband allowed her for food. A letter requested the preacher to use the fund to provide her child with a few bits of finery

such as are due any girl just budding into womanhood.

Along came the Easter season, when the local milliner displayed in her window a hat that she had imported from New York. It created a furor among the ladies of the village and so fascinated our heroine that every day she repaired to the window of the shop to gape at it in awe and longing. On Easter Sunday, who showed up in church wearing the elaborate concoction? Why, that penniless heroine. The gossipy milliner on being quizzed, announced that the hat had been purchased by their young bachelor clergyman.

Rumors of an illicit affair between the two grew to a point where a good girl's reputation was tottering and the preacher was about to be unfrocked. Naturally, justice prevailed when the mother's deathbed letter was produced and the heroine's father revealed as a niggardly tyrant. In fact, the preacher even went so far as to take a swipe at the entire community for its snide New England prejudices. But the scandal brought its victims together in a way that would ultimately end in marriage.

(*The New York Hat,* as a particularly fine example of Griffith's direction, is still shown at the Museum of Modern Art in New York. It is also run sometimes on television. And it was through seeing *The New York Hat* that David Belasco decided to put Mary Pickford into the title role of his Broadway production of *A Good Little Devil.*)

In a way, this film, *The New York Hat*, came to influence the Broadway stage. David Belasco was about to produce a play called *A Good Little Devil*. He was looking for a young actress for the title role, and someone steered him into a movie theater where he saw *The New York Hat*. Mary's performance convinced Belasco, who forthwith transferred Mary Pickford to the Broadway stage. It was to be her last appearance in the theater. From that point on, Mary went all the way in films.

Bored with acting in the San Diego stock company, I continued to write film plots. The majority were slapstick comedies that ended in a chase by Keystone Kops. I mailed them to the Biograph Studio in New York at the rate of one or two a month.

One day I received a letter dated "New York, January 6, 1914." In that letter, I was addressed as "Madam," for success had made me bold enough to take a chance on adding the feminine "Anita" to my name. Dougherty's letter informed me that the Biograph Company was moving west. He wrote, "We will be located in Hollywood, and I'd like to have a personal interview with you at our Studio on the corner of Georgia and Gerard Streets."

I was overcome by a curiosity to meet the shadowy characters who were acting in my scripts. So I talked Mother into taking the trip and, chaperoned by her as always, we entered a world of the most fabulous mummery ever devised by man.

As our streetcar entered Hollywood, we found it to be a dilapidated suburb, which was climaxed at the end of the line

D.W. was the first director ever to rehearse a scene before the cameras started to grind. We would all assemble around him, and anybody's suggestion was listened to. Deep in the shadow is Billy Bitzer, who was more responsible for raising film photography to the realm of art than any other cameraman of his day.

23

by the old Hollywood Hotel, a rambling edifice painted the same dust color of the hills. On the veranda, elderly seekers after sunshine sat in big red chairs and rocked their uneventful lives away. Across from the hotel was a shabby business district, and there were a few bungalows interspersed with vacant lots. Nobody ever dreamed that a day was close at hand when Hollywood would express both sex and sin in their most delectable forms.

There was no reason why Hollywood should ever have been named in honor of a shrub that can only exist in a cold climate. But legend had it that a couple of oldsters from England had come there, built a fine house, and, in nostalgia for their homeland, planted a slip of holly in the garden. Before it had time to wither in the hot dry air, they caused the name "Hollywood" to be painted on the front gate. Thus was Hollywood christened with a name as spurious as anything that would ever come out of its studios.

The Biograph Studio consisted of a row of one story shacks. On the center door was painted "Biograph Company—Main Office." Mother, ordinarily so timid, forged on ahead of me. She must have sensed that she was in danger of losing forever her "Honeybunch," and wanted to investigate what sort of world it was that might gobble me up.

For that first encounter with Fate, I had snobbishly copied the good taste of

European royalty and was dressed in a white linen sailor suit, with my hair in a long braid tied with black taffeta bows. In the flashy locale we were about to enter, I must have seemed like a school-child of about twelve.

We came into a long, low, narrow office, partitioned by a counter, behind which two minor employees were engaged in desultory conversation. One of them asked what we wanted, and Mother spoke up to say Miss Loos was there to see Mr. Dougherty. Polite but not very interested, the man told us to take a seat, and then disappeared through the back doorway.

Presently a large Irish-American in a seersucker suit emerged and, mistaking Mother for the authoress, approached her. "Well, Mrs. Loos!" said he genially, "it's nice to meet you after all this time."

At which Mother corrected him. "But I'm Anita's mother. This is Anita Loos."

Dougherty turned a look of blank amazement on me; and before he could get over his surprise that those satiric comedies had been written by a child, a door opened and the movie's first real genius emerged into view from the back lot.

Up to that time, David Wark Griffith had been merely a name scrawled on vouchers that came by mail. Most of my correspondence had been with Dougherty, who, to my mind, was the more important of two unknowns.

Griffith was tall, bronzed, and rangy like a cowboy. He was in his shirt sleeves and wore a battered straw sombrero tied under his chin with a black shoe lace. But his ridiculous get-up didn't detract one bit from D.W.'s enormous distinction. He must have been in his early thirties, but he had an authority that seemed to deny he had ever been young. His high arched nose belonged on some Roman emperor; his pale eyes, in sharp contrast to the tan of his complexion, sparkled with a sort of archaic amusement, as if he were constantly saying to himself, "What fools these mortals be."

But that morning, it was Griffith's turn to be fooled. Bypassing me, he advanced to shake Mother's hand as Dougherty had done. At which the latter spoke up to say, "You're shaking hands with the *mother* of our authoress. It's this little lady who's been writing our slapstick farces."

Turning to look at me, Griffith's expression went as blank as had Dougherty's. I sensed that it was my childish appearance that stunned them into silence, but I managed to stammer that I was pleased to meet them. After which there didn't seem to be anything more to say. And then Mother, relieved to save her child, spoke up. "Goodbye gentlemen," she said. "Come along, Honeybunch."

We walked out of that office with Mother feeling we had escaped from a tribe of savages, while the brevity of their welcome had made me feel frustrated and bitterly disappointed. We had gone about half a block toward the streetcar line, when we heard a booming voice call, "Miss Looze." (Griffith had an affectation of mispronouncing words. He never did or said anything in the same manner as other people. And that bond between the two of us remained invincible. I had met someone after my own dissident heart.)

Then, looking me over, D.W. announced that he wanted to put me into the film he was directing. But I had had my fill of being an actress, playing in trumped up situations, repeating second-hand speeches. I adored finding myself in the haphazard situations of real life, where I could make up my own on-the-spot dialogue.

So that cliché, "You ought to be in pictures," even when spoken by an expert, didn't tempt me. It was just as well —I was far from the "Griffith type." Had I been required to play one of his typical heroines; dodging around the furniture to escape some libertine, I'd have instantly ducked out of sight under the bed, and the scene would have ended in anticlimax.

I still have an account book with a record of my early scripts; between the years of 1912 and 1915 there were 105 of them, of which only four were rejected by the Biograph Company. But the rejects found a ready market at the Vitagraph, Kalem, or Selig studios.

I never kept copies of those plots, but I remember one called *A Girl Like Mother*.

Watching my studio chums cavort in *Intolerance* inspired me in 1924 to give the heroine of *G.P.B.* a brief career in the movies. A description by Lorelei Lee herself reads, "I played the girl who fainted when a lot of gentlemen fell off a tower."

When my fiancé John Emerson and I collaborated, he saw to it that the publicity cameras recorded every minor incident.

Its heroine is a young lady who is having trouble landing her beau because the young man is hellbent on marrying "a girl like mother." So it crosses our heroine's mind to look up her intended mother-in-law, study the woman surreptitiously, and then give an imitation of her. But in looking up "Mother," our heroine is given a wrong steer by a hated rival, and the woman she studies can only be termed a harridan. As a result, her imitation is catastrophic. But she must have landed a husband at the end, or the film would have been a tragedy.

There was a melodrama, *Saved by the Soup*, in which my heroine is a beautiful spy in the U.S. Secret Service. While at a banquet in Washington, our spy overhears a plot that will bring disaster to her native land. It may already be too late for the heroine to save the U.S.A. However, at this juncture luck steps into the script, for our quick-witted spy glances into a dish the butler sets before her, sees that it contains alphabet soup, and immediately spells out "Call the cops" on the edge of her plate. The butler loses no time in sounding the alarm; the famous Keystone Kops are summoned, and, during a wild chase, in which pies contribute their custard to the shambles, the U.S.A. is saved.

A script in which Fay Tincher played

27

Nellie, the Female Villain had more romantic overtones. Nellie is a girl from the Far West who on her arrival in London is invited to an aristocratic ball. She reaches there only to learn that her Western attire is provocative of japes from the high-class ladies of British nobility. But Nellie was not raised in Texas for nothing. Stationing herself in the entrance hall, she looks over the girls as they arrive, chooses a victim who wears a Paris gown, shoves her into the ladies' room, pulls out a gun, makes her disrobe, puts on her dress, and then emerges to become the belle of the ball. And that very night she lands a royal duke for her affianced husband.

Frequently I came through with more serious plots. One of these, *The Wild Girl of the Sierras*, brought a check for $100 (prices were going up!).

I wrote another tragedy called *Stranded*, for which I received $300 (prices were beginning to soar). I wrote *Stranded* for the aging Broadway star DeWolf Hopper, who had just married a willowy young brunette named Hedda. The plot concerned a ham actor who had always yearned to play Shakespeare, but nobody would give him the chance. Finally, during a tour of the Wild West, he becomes the innocent victim of gunplay in a saloon. And while he lies dying on the barroom floor (in the midst of a goodly crowd), he grasps the opportunity to recite, "Friends, Romans, countrymen, lend me your ears," et cetera. Seeing that nobody has the heart to stop him, the poor

It is sad to inject this note of tragedy—the location shot for D.W.'s last movie, *The Struggle*. The story took place in the New York slums; and, just as the first movie I ever wrote had been directed by D.W., I was to write his last one. By that time, D.W. had come to grief. After providing fortunes for the innumerable stars he created, D.W. was broke; he had lost all his money by investing in his own movies.

The film was a failure, thereby adding to D.W.'s drinking problem, which had reached its most destructive level. And this was the sad end of a history-making career.

Fay dominated my slapstick comedies for several years, but we were never very close. It was different with Mabel Normand. I loved her. She was as energetic in creating mischief as she was lazy when it came to work.

In the days when Mabel Normand was a co-star with Mack Sennett's Keystone Kops, Mack used to send his car for her in the mornings. The driver would honk; Mabel would appear at the window and say, "I'll be there in a minute." After which she would slither back into bed and lose herself in slumber for the remainder of the morning.

old boy gives the only Shakespearean performance of his career and enjoys a happy death.

The plots I wrote in the beginning were pretty contrived, but as my experience with life broadened, I began to dredge real situations and real people from it. I wrote a picture for Douglas Fairbanks called *American Aristocracy*, which was a satire on the big names of United States industry, such as the Fords, the Heinzes of pickle fame, and the Chalmerses, who were touchingly proud of the underwear they manufactured.

Trashy as those old plots were, they were acted with a gusto that has disappeared from Hollywood and explains the present cult for early films. Mack Sennett, the Daddy of all slapstick farce, W.C. Fields, Mae West, and Charlie Chaplin have a definite kinship with Molière.

The heroines of many of my half-reel farces were played by Fay Tincher, who has now been long forgotten. Ideal for those rowdy scripts, Fay required no acting ability. Let's say that she had the pert allure of a "Patsy" and could be a provocative target for slapstick. Fay was anything but a sex symbol, and—in those days before lesbians came out of the closet—her fans never dreamed that their rambunctious little idol harbored a preference for g-i-r-l-s!

Mabel Normand, at the other end of the spectrum, had the tantalizing sex appeal of a scamp. A wild and naughty girl, she was a pioneer in drug addiction long before it took Hollywood by storm. In her early days, Mabel was loved by a rising young movie mogul named Samuel Goldwyn. She made fun of Sam (as who didn't?), and she adored the producer of her madcap films, Mack Sennet. In 1974, David Merrick produced a musical on Broadway in the memory of that love affair. But a musical comedy in which the heroine is carried off by drugs in the prime of her youth and beauty put audiences into low spirits, and the show flopped. I couldn't bear to see it. I loved Mabel; she was one of my favorite outlaws.

But the most pathetic gamin of all those early Griffith pictures was Mae Marsh. Off-screen Mae shared my pretensions of being stylish and artistic. Mae's sister Marguerite was *really* stylish, but she harbored no pretensions to culture. While still young and beautiful, Marguerite joined Mabel Normand in a fatal destiny of drug addiction.

Mae Marsh had a heartbreaking quality on-screen that inspired one of my few attempts at being serious. A picture titled *The Little Liar* got us both an accolade from the poet Vachel Lindsay. He wrote a poem to Mae, but when the three of us met, she found that Vachel bore an unfortunate resemblance to the ventriloquist dummy Mortimer Snerd created by Edgar Bergen. Mae's indifference caused the poet to switch his devotion to me; and, over the years, he wrote me love letters, which now repose in the Houghton Museum at Harvard.

This blonde leading lady later made history, just like Helen of Troy. In Doug's troupe, she behaved like an angel; but when she moved on to another studio, it suddenly transpired that she had not yet reached the legal age of consent. The entire studio had to move across the border and resume filming in Mexico.

Those P.R. cameras never ceased to function. They recorded for posterity a well-known trio of star, scenarist, and director.

There were two outstanding stars of silent films who happened to be sisters: Norma and Constance Talmadge. I wrote movies for them both. The mother of those girls, known as Peg, manipulated her two beauties into the top ranks of both films and finance. But Peg's preference was for the latter. Among Norma's many husbands, the first was the movie tycoon Joseph Schenck. He was followed by Georgie Jessel, of equal eminence as a stand-up comedian. Norma's other husbands and lovers were also rich but far from tiresome.

Constance Talmadge, known as "Dutch" (a hoyden as well as a beauty), could have married any man who ever met her. Irving Thalberg, Irving Berlin, and Dick Barthelmess waxed suicidal over her indifference. And the men she *did* marry continued to adore Dutch long after divorces parted them.

Peg's third daughter Natalie wasn't beautiful enough for the movies, so Peg married her off to Buster Keaton. Buster Keaton! Born of vaudevillian parents; raised in show-biz, as was another commentator on the human scene several centuries ago. Keaton was a sort of mini-Molière, and like the great French dramatist, a genius and a poet.

The wedding of Buster and Natalie took place at the estate of Joe Schenck in Great Neck, Long Island. On that occasion, Peg's smile was forced; she considered Natalie's marriage as a mere substitute for movie stardom. I disagreed.

Mae Marsh became a silent-movie star, while her sister Marguerite settled for fun and games in the early drug invasion of Hollywood. Mae inspired a poem by Vachel Lindsay, which now lies in the archives of the Houghton Museum at Harvard.

Norma Talmadge, a vibrant brunette, epitomized the tragedy inherent in too much sex appeal.

Every male who ever met Constance Talmadge fell for her. The list includes Irving Thalberg, Irving Berlin, and Richard Barthelmess. She lived to marry four of her many suitors, who never ceased to lament the day she divorced them.

Peg Talmadge married off her ugly duckling, Natalie, to Buster Keaton. The ceremony took place at Joe Schenck's estate in Great Neck, Long Island. Constance was matron of honor, in which post she was bolstered by her first husband, John Pialagalou, one of the first rich Greeks to enter the matrimonial sweepstakes of the U.S.A.

To the far left is A.L.; next to me, the mother of the bride; then Norma, next to whom is the groom. In the background Norma's husband, Joe Schenck, with a few assorted V.I.P.'s of the movie world.

That marriage turned one of the world's great clowns into a figure of tragedy.

I used to think that looking across a pillow into the fabulous face of Buster Keaton would be a more thrilling destiny than any screen career.

My wedding to John Emerson, who was the director of Constance's films, duplicated Buster's and Natalie's in taking place at Joe Schenck's Great Neck estate. Joe was John's best man; Frances Marion, the scenarist, was maid of honor, and all the movie bigshots in the New York area were present.

I had set my sights on a man of brains, to whom I could look up. But what a terrible let down it would be to find out that I was smarter than he was.

The Emersons were rich due to the booming stock market of the Twenties. We were able to quit Hollywood and a social life that was restricted to the caste system of the studios. Our lives could have become a protracted honeymoon had we both happened to enjoy the same things. The trouble was that we didn't. Although we shared a love for New York and made the city a home base between frequent visits abroad, John's sole interest was the New York theater. He went to plays seven nights a week, dragging me along when I could have been sitting in some lowly bistro with such wits as H.L. Mencken and George Jean Nathan, the theater critic who had a knowledge of Ibsen and Strindberg even before their plays were done on Broadway.

But what of the Algonquin Round Table,

The Emersons' wedding at the Great Neck estate of Joe Schenck, was a replica of the Keatons', with any number of our cronies present. With such a fascinating group of fellow travelers, it should have been an ideal marriage. But instead of living happily ever after, John and I set about wrecking each other's lives. Our marriage was both tragic and comic, together with a thousand combinations of the two.

one might ask. The truth was that I found their exhibitionism pretty naïve. It did not impress me to listen when Alec Woollcott would ask Heywood Broun, "Do you recall that brilliant crack I made to Dottie Parker when F.P.A. accused me of cheating at croquet with Herbert Swope?" The spending of each other's names made their minds rather a closed circuit.

Menck's lack of interest in the Round Table had caused him to remark, "their ideals were those of a vaudeville actor; one who is extremely 'in the know' and inordinately trashy."

At the time I met Menck, he was in his early forties; a bachelor who made his home in Baltimore, occupying the house where he was born. He spent no more time in New York than the few days each month required as co-publisher with George Jean Nathan of the *Smart Set*. His preference for Baltimore was because, in his own words, "it bulged with normalcy."

Menck's writings had made him a matinee idol on every college campus. Had he wished, he could have enjoyed the romantic success of which his elegant *confrère* George Jean Nathan boasted and Scott Fitzgerald wrote. It was only natural that Menck's attractions overcame a

In the beginning of their association, Mencken and Nathan were inseparable. I adored Mencken, but George was easier to hook. So I took him on, as many a New York cutie did, because he preferred small females who made him appear taller than he actually was.

cerebral flapper like me.

I soon learned that, during Menck's short visits to New York, he was too busy to be hooked, but his partner George Jean Nathan was easy. George's handsome pomposity didn't match his short stature, and I was tiny enough for him to look over my head. So I took him on to enjoy second-hand the crumbs of wit he picked up from Mencken and made a career of repeating.

Ultimately a miracle took place. I began to be invited by Herman Oelrichs, a cultured socialite, to a hideaway Herman kept in the east fifties. It was the real center of the New York intelligentsia of that day. There I came to know such talents as Theodore Dreiser, Sherwood Anderson, and Ernest Boyd, the Irish essayist. (Ernest bore a great resemblance to the pictures of Christ. And he once wrote on a photograph he sent to me, "What a friend you have in Jesus.")

While Emerson was disporting among the folks of show biz, I was listening first hand to Henry Mencken. I had found an idol to adore for a lifetime.

In my peregrinations in and out of movie studios and the nightlife of New York and other world capitals we happened to cover, it might seem that I was partial to men, which is true enough. But, along the way, I found girl friends who were so enormously sympathetic that, except for those who are no longer around, we're still close today. The common denominator that brought us together was the fun we had in living.

A fashion photographer once tricked me into posing for this in Coronado. At the same time, he was photographing a reigning Coronado belle—a navy bride named Wallis Warfield who was to go on to wreck a dynasty.

3

THE GIRLS

A fashionable group gathered for lunch at the Ritz Hotel in Paris. At the far right is Elinor Glyn, who had just published her naughty novel *Three Weeks*. At the far left is Elinor's sister, Lady Duff Gordon, who operated chic dressmaking salons in London and New York. She is flanked by John Emerson and his little bride, who was more intrigued by a bit of gossip concerning the Duff Gordons than in their august titles—it was hinted that during the sinking of the *Titanic*, His Lordship had donned one of his wife's negligees and obeyed the summons, "Ladies and children first."

On a bright day in the mid-thirties, Mrs. Eddie Duchin, Leopold Stokowski, and I disported at my beach home in Santa Monica. Eddie, who was touring the U.S. with his dance-band, had taken his bride along, and now his engagement at the Ambassador Hotel in Los Angeles gave Marge and me a chance to renew our friendship, which had begun in the haunts of café society around the world.

Stokie and I were both on salary at M.G.M., where I was writing movie scripts and he was experimenting with an idea to introduce music into films in a new and arbitrary manner. (M.G.M. didn't appreciate Stokie, and, when his idea ultimately came through, it was for Walt Disney in the film *Fantasia*).

Stokie took a bemused interest in my group of girl friends. We had all been obscure in early youth, but were now on our way to prominence along widely divergent lines. Marge's celebrity had come by being ousted from the New York Social Register for leaving the prominent Oelrichs family to marry society's hotshot bandleader. It was all right for Marge's cousin Herman to hobnob with rowdy thinkers like Mencken, but a nice Park Avenue debutante mustn't hang out at the Park Casino listening to ragtime.

Another member of our clique was Adele Astaire who, as Lady Cavendish, was to desert her fame as the sister and dancing partner of Fred, by marrying Lord Cavendish and keeping house in Ireland's grandest castle. Then there was Ruth

43

Obré, later the Countess de Vallombrosa, who was holding forth at a townhouse on the Avenue Foch in Paris. Ina Claire was injecting high comedy into musical shows as no other American actress has ever done. Helen Hayes requires no additional description. Tilly Losch was an internationally famous dancer before she ever married Lord Carnarvon, who financed the excavation of Tutankhamen's tomb. Not the least contributor to that odd social upheaval was Foxie Armstrong, who had married the Earl of Sefton, multi-millionaire sportsman and owner of the racetrack at Aintree where the Grand National is run.

One day Stokie said to me, "You ought to write something about that extraordinary group of Cinderellas."

Well Stokie, here goes!

Back in the Twenties, Foxie Armstrong was modeling clothes in New York when the French couturier, Patou, arrived there, on a quest for American beauties on whom he could exhibit his dresses to American customers. Of all those New York lovelies, Foxie was Patou's first choice.

As the prettiest redhead in Paris, Foxie promptly married a young member of the Vanderbilt clan, Willie Gwynn. But Willie, alas, belonged to a poor branch of the Vanderbilts and Foxie continued to work. After Willie's early death, she caught the eye of one of England's richest peers, the Earl of Sefton. Foxie became his Countess and then, during World War II, the Earl was elected Lord Mayor of Liverpool.

Marjorie Duchin and I were to learn that Leopold Stokowski was a prophet as well as a great conductor.

44

In Paris, Marge, Ruth, and I once posed for this nice, clean version of a French postcard.

Adele didn't need to keep her feet on the ground in order to enter the British aristocracy as Lady Cavendish.

Foxie outfoxed all us girls when she became Lady Mayoress of Liverpool.

The famed astronomer Edwin Hubble, his wife Grace, my niece Mary, Chaplin, Emerson, and Tilly Losch.

I tagged along with the Irving Berlins on their honeymoon at Baden-Baden.

At this period, Ruth Obré-Goldbeck-de Vallombrosa-Dubonnet was the Countess de Vallombrosa. She bore two nicknames given her by chic Parisians. The Count de Chambrum dubbed her "Panthère," because of her streamlined grace and Prince Bibesco called her "Animal de Luxe." The Vallombrosas were considered the best-looking couple in Paris.

Another of our group, Ruth Obré-Goldbeck-de Vallombrosa-Dubonnet, began her career in Washington, D.C. She had gone there to trade the tedium of small-town life in upstate New York for the excitement of Washington during World War I, which she herself helped to glamorize as a stenographer. Ruthie's beauty and gay spirits were soon discovered by Walter Goldbeck, the most fashionable portrait painter of the Twenties. Ruth married Walter and let him guide her up the next step on the social ladder. He took his bride to Europe and introduced her to the smart sets of its various capitals. When I first met Ruthie, she had become the Countess de Vallombrosa. We visited and giggled together at her townhouse in Paris and an ancestral estate in the Midi.

During the summer of '24, Foxie, Ruthie, Dellie, Tilly, Marge, and I were all in Paris, riding high on the dizzy predilection the French had, in happier days, for everything American. In café society, the shots were called by Elsa Maxwell. We all trailed after her, danced the Charleston to the music of ragtime, smoked cigarettes in long holders, and

Dominating the Vallombrosa's Paris salon was the Countess' portrait by her first husband, Walter Goldbeck. While the Count was extremely jealous, he paid no attention to art, so it's possible he never knew who painted Ruthie's portrait.

MONSIEUR F. W.

dans l'exercice
de ses fonctions.

Paris in the Twenties
was best described by
the sketches of our
friend, the caricaturist
Sem.

"Why should'nt
I look like a doll too?"

"What a crime!"

50

revealed the human knee for the first time since ancient Romans dressed in togas. Paris in the Twenties was *très gai!* But the job of describing it is best turned over to that French artist who went by the nom-de-plume of "Sem."

Now I, myself, had recently described Fanny Ward, the aging playgirl and actress, as having been "cute for eighty years." Sem, with a few strokes of his crayon, did a better job.

Fanny was married to a youngish fellow traveler in that giddy world. His name was Jack Dean and, from the chin up he was handsome enough, but from the chin down Jack's profile lacked definition. So Fanny, as a devoted helpmeet, unearthed a cosmetic surgeon who had invented a process of injecting wax into areas that were scanty, and he provided Jack with a masterful, cleancut jaw that would have

"o on, then, you executioner!"

"But i dont look like a doll at all. I look like the Comtesse de S.... rte, Damn'it!"

A great lady emerged
out of the brouhaha of the Twenties—
Linda Porter.

done honor to the sculptures on Mount Rushmore.

And then disaster struck! The plastic surgeon hadn't mastered a technique to prevent wax from melting in warm weather. So Jack's manly jaw slipped several inches south of where it should have been.

Jack's mishap gave rise to numberless quips among our coterie. Doug Fairbanks dubbed him "Chin-Chin" after a current play. Dotty Parker, paraphrasing the title of another play *Three Faces East*, nicknamed Jack "*Two* Faces East."

But it was Sem who surmounted us all in levity, by portraying Jack as a doting nursemaid to his Sugar Mamma. Paris in the Twenties could also be *très admirable*.

There is little perfection in this vale of tears and, again to quote from *Gentlemen Prefer Blondes*; "A girl can't go on laughing all the time." As proof of which I offer Linda Porter.

When Cole Porter married Linda, she was the wealthy divorcee of a New York newspaper owner. Linda was the elder by several years, and their relationship was that of the permissive Mamma and a very naughty son. For Cole led a life that was far above good or evil.

The fact that Linda suffered from lung trouble gave Cole plenty of opportunity to roam. She spent her latter years in New York, where her apartment at the Waldorf Towers was equipped to be an oversized oxygen tent. To visit Linda in

Cole sometimes wasted his peerless lyrics on a pooch.

IN THE LOUNGE OF

THE HOTEL INCROYABLE.

Punch Almanack 1929. Reprinted by permission of *Punch* magazine and Rothco Cartoons.

that rarefied air was a heady experience, even in the clean New York of those days.

Linda's doctors allowed her only one visitor at a time, so we took turns in lunching with her. One time when Cole was in Hollywood, mixing business with pleasure at the M.G.M. studio, I suggested that Linda, for a change, might risk a trip into the pure air of Atlantic City. "Oh I'll never leave the Waldorf," Linda replied so emphatically that I asked why. "Because we're just across from St. Bartholomew's. And when time comes for those last rites, Coley may be far away but, once he gets here, he'll have very little further to go."

It was at St. Bartholomew's a few months later that Coley said the last of his many goodbyes to Linda.

It was a refresher to one's spirit that any member of our razzmatazz milieu could be so saintly.

Howard Sturges constituted another of Linda Porter's martyrdoms. He had been born to both wealth and culture, being a nephew of our foremost American philosopher, George Santayana. In Howard's gilded youth, he had joined the clique surrounding Cole Porter. But Cole's genius provided him with an occupation, whereas Sturgie's only genius was for fun. (In his Uncle George's autobiography, *The Last Puritan*, he tells of Sturgie being a prodigious party-giver; "at the same time a host and hostess," wrote Uncle George.)

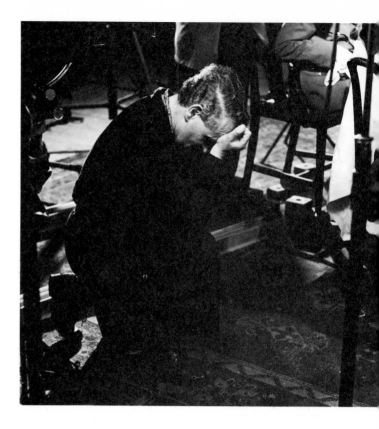

Well, while Cole was scaling the heights of luxury, Sturgie hit the gutters of Paris with the mighty thud of drug addiction. And there Linda found Sturgie, picked him out of the depths and kept him straight for the remainder of her life.

Sturgie's reformation was not quite so revolutionary as that of St. Anthony of Padua. For his only religion was to worship Linda Porter. But Sturgie also kept his friendship with Cole intact.

On a side trip to London, Viscount D'Abernon introduced me to all the "right" people in Britain. His Lordship had been a member of the British Commission sent to Berlin to work out peace conditions following World War II,

Puffin Asquith on his movie set, puzzling over a forthcoming scene. Puff had deserted his status as son of the wartime Prime Minister and his witty helpmeet, Margot, for a career in the studios.

Cecil Beaton sketched me and my swain, Viscount D'Abernon, on a stroll down Piccadilly.

an afternoon with Dab.

and he had written a memoir entitled *An Ambassador of Peace*.

It amused Lord D'Abernon to consult me about his manuscript and, when it was published, I found the dedication to read: "To the fairest of all critics." He had used the word "fair" as a synonym for "comely" and a subtle compliment.

His Lordship's appearance had always seemed vaguely familiar; and, long after his death, I met an English expatriate living in Baltimore who informed me that my British beau was an illegitimate son of King Edward VII by a Spanish dancer who worked in the London music halls.

Anthony Asquith's father was Lord Oxford, who had been England's Prime Minister during World War I; his mother was the witty and caustic Margot; his sister, Princess Bibesco, was an outstanding poet. The Asquiths welcomed me into their family circle, in which there never was heard a cliché.

The aristocracy used to affect silly nicknames, so Margot had called her son "Puffin" when he was a baby, and he remained "Puffin" after he became a distinguished film director.

With wealth and leisure, John Emerson took to social-climbing. And during the winter seasons, all the right people betook themselves to Florida. I hated the idea of leaving a beloved lifestyle of the world capitals we'd been occupying to sink into the gilded apathy of Palm Beach. But John was adamant, and as usual I complied, at the same time

57

Café society moved to Palm Beach every winter, and life went on apace.

On the opposite page, a dress in two shades of green, designed by Yvonne Davidson, wife of the sculptor Jo.

revolted by that Southern culture that seemed to be as desolate as that of Arkansas, which Mencken had branded "The Sahara of the Beaux Arts," which Menck spelled "Bozarts."

I was revolted entering the life of Palm Beach. But ensconced in the nullity of Palm Beach social life, I was to learn, with an optimism worthy of my angelic mother, that it's always darker just before the dawn. In simple terms, I met up with the first successor to Henry Mencken I'd found, to date. His wit was unorthodox, and he only used it for the fun of living. His name was Wilson Mizner.

Wilson Mizner was born with an intellect that could have masterminded all the complexities of high finance. But early in life, he began to feel that such pursuits might lack amusement. So at seventeen he deserted the conservative family estate which was located across the Bay from San Francisco, to invade the Barbary Coast— that section of the city famous the world over for a wholehearted dedication to pleasure. There Wilson took up headquarters in a gambling casino, where he dealt a card game called faro and became a wealthy teenager, long before the rock stars of today.

From that brisk beginning, Wilson forged north to Alaska in the heyday of its gold rush and, in its pioneer saloons, gambled with prospectors for their hard-earned nuggets and bags of gold dust.

Then, longing for more urbane fleshpots, Wilson went east to New York, at a time when its girls wore gorgeous dresses and when blue jeans were strictly the garb of plumbers and pipe fitters. There, Wilson was pressured into writing a melodrama about the underworld he knew so well. Entitled *The Deep Purple*, it became the Broadway hit of its season and made Wilson his first legitimate fortune. But disdaining the sedentary life of an author, Wilson was seduced by the frenzied real-estate boom down in Florida. He joined the gold rush to Palm Beach where he succeeded in turning its salubrious clime into a racket. Wilson stacked up another fortune, selling vacant lots through the mail to purchasers far and wide, who didn't know that their homesites lay several inches beneath the blue Atlantic.

At length, the law dragged Wilson into

One weekend, we slipped away from Palm Beach and, accompanied by Wilson's gambling pal, "The Elk City Flash," went to Havana for fun and profit. Batista was in power then; and, as a professional courtesy to Wilson and "The Flash," we all won at roulette in the Casino.

Wilson Mizner, a modern Robin Hood, robbed the rich to give to the unworthy poor. His heart bled for all derelicts who were down on their luck. Henry Mencken envied me my friendship with Wilson. "I wish I'd known him," said Menck. "He was a sweet guy."

60

Palm Beach was invented by Addison Mizner. As an architect, he infused it with glamour and then reigned over it with the benevolence of a King Cole. Among his merry subjects were Ray Goetz (impresario of Cole Porter's musicals) and Herbert and Minnie Weston, pets of Park Avenue Society.

Like all the Mizner clan, Wilson's nephew Horace lived a life out-of-bounds. Horace and I would attend the Palm Beach parties that Wilson disdained, but our motive was to make fun of them. As a dilettante pilot, I used to go flying with him, until I learned his plane had only rudimentary landing gear. The next week on a solo trip, Horace's plane crashed, leaving no survivor.

court, where an irate Judge demanded, "Didn't you assure your victims they could grow nuts on their land?" To which Wilson replied, "My investors misunderstood, sir. What I said was that they could *go* nuts on their land." Following which rejoinder, Wilson managed to get out on bail, which he jumped to flee across the state line, just ahead of a sheriff.

Wilson then headed west to spend his final years in Hollywood during its inception as the world's most enchanting source of easy money.

One night, toward the end of his life, Wilson was in the bar at the Brown Derby with Darryl Zanuck, then head of production at Warner Brothers. During their chitchat, Wilson casually ad-libbed the plot for a movie. That film, entitled *One Way Passage*, earned an Academy Award after Wilson's death. It was sad to think how deeply Wilson would have cherished that accolade from Hollywood's most flamboyant racket.

Wilson's dialogue, written down on paper, now seems either vulgar or obscene, but his courtly manner invested it with a bizarre sort of elegance. He was credited with the saying, "Always treat a lady like a whore and a whore like a lady," but he accorded the most besotted females and the most conservative matrons the same genteel respect. Wilson, in fact, had a tender compassion toward all mankind, which—to his mind—had been trapped in a world full

John was sketched by James Montgomery Flagg, whose talent was generally devoted to cover-girls like Zsa Zsa Gabor. Flagg's portrait of John now hangs in the Players Club in New York in memory of the great job John did in the actors' strike of 1919.

"SEE THE PLAYERS WELL BESTOWED"

Addison was sketched by Cecil Beaton in a special outsized chair he designed. "It's big enough to put Nita to bed in," Addie used to say.

of woe, where an innocent party like himself, intent only on enjoying life, was affronted by the backlash of drug addiction and V.D.

Wilson's dialogue had much in common with that of W.C. Fields. But he also spoke with the classical elegance written into the dialogue of Falstaff by Will Shakespeare. And, unlike most wits, Wilson was as good a listener as he was a talker. How else could he have picked up the knowledge of human frailty that turned his con games into demonstrations of applied psychology.

Books have been written about him and a movie based on his life is now in preparation. But the actor who plays Wilson must have the charisma of Robert Redford, the braggadocio of Frank Sinatra, and the outrageousness of Murph the Surf.

I cite an occasion at the Ambassador Hotel in Los Angeles. Wilson hadn't long to live, and he lay fighting for breath in an oxygen tank. I went to visit him every day, sometimes accompanied by our mutual friend Mark Kelly, a sportswriter on the Los Angeles *Times*. Mark was a devout Catholic, and the last time we were ever to see Wilson, Mark brought along a crucifix to hang over his bed. Cocking a skeptical eye at it, Wilson wheezed, "So you think that thing can postpone the Main Event, do you?" "I know it can!" answered Mark. "But look at the fix that poor guy got into *himself*," said Wilson.

I knew that Wilson in all the locales he had inhabited except Alaska; that sad omission being that I hadn't been born yet. I first met him in Palm Beach, where I was enthralled by the aura of his adventurous past and the challenge of his being an unsuitable companion for the child bride of a gentleman of esteem in the theater.

Our situation, like most of life's verities, can be best described in a cliché. It was stronger than we were.

The photograph of the Palm Beach dinner party brings to light a foolish joke that took place in that silliest of all pleasure resorts, Palm Beach. The butt of our joke was the eminent novelist, Joseph Hergesheimer. Now Joe had just written two best sellers, *Java Head* and *The Three Black Pennys*; he could have basked in the acclaim of both fans and critics, but he was obsessed by dreams of entering a snob's fairyland as a seasoned man of the world. So dear old Joe would make passionate love to several girls at a party, unaware that on meeting in the powder room, we'd swap jokes about our suitor.

It was considerate of Joe that he restricted his lovemaking to dialogue, because two of his front teeth were totally missing and the others too snaggled for use.

One winter when Joe ventured to join the exodus from New York to Palm Beach,

he had timorously asked Henry Mencken,
"Do you think I might be invited to one of
the more exclusive parties down there?"
And Menck had promptly phoned Addison
Mizner to ask, "Will you please get Joe
into some nest of Palm Beach snobs
and make the little man happy?"

Now the Florida resort, then as always,
was largely inhabited by phonies, but there
were a few bona fide aristocrats around,
so Addison invited them for a dinner
in Joe's honor. And then, because Addie
knew that Marjorie Oelrichs and I were
recipients of Joe's favor, he turned further
arrangements over to us.

We were all for making Joe happy, but
at the same time we resented the

Addison gave a dinner.
Among the guests are Joseph
Hergesheimer, Princess Anita
Lobkowitz, John Emerson, the
Vicomte de Frise, Mrs. Herbert
Weston, Baron Somebody-or-other,
Anita Loos, and Addison Mizner,
whose expression reveals his shame
at being an accessory to the caper.

66

romantic two-timing he had inflicted on us, and we decided to inject a dash of the bitter into his triumph. In planning the menu, we selected items for which front teeth are indispensable; artichokes, corn on the cob, and, to the bewilderment of a classy Palm Beach butcher, filet mignon that must be guaranteed for toughness. Dessert was to be decked out with a caramel sauce that created an uneatable web of sticky goo.

Addison, as host, began to be bewildered by the behavior of his guests who were putting on a lot of regal schmaltz; ladies curtsied to Joe as if he were a monarch, and Joe, taking it in stride, kissed ladies' hands in a sort of deep, undercover ecstasy.

Our small talk concerned royal personages who were called by familiar names; the Prince of Wales was "David," and there were any number of others;—"Bibi," "Dodo," "Poopsie," etc. When a photographer arrived to take the picture for the society page of the Palm Beach *News*, Addie finally realized what we had been up to.

But Joe's acceptance of his honors is still evident in his benign expression, and the rest of us could excuse ourselves that, for one glorious evening, our dear old Joe had occupied a high post in dreamland. I feel I can expertize on the subject of con men, because I later came to know Mussolini while in Rome for an international conference of theater folk.

In Mussolini's Rome, there was an Englishwoman whom I shall designate as Lady Jones. Her duties were to teach *Il Duce* English and to translate for him. Her Ladyship introduced herself to me one day at the Excelsior Hotel and announced that *Il Duce* wished to meet me, unencumbered by conventioneers. As I reacted, properly impressed, she continued. "But His Excellency can never tell in advance if he'll be free. So if you'll be in the hotel each afternoon at five, I'll phone to let you know if the interview can take place."

Now, I had just been equipped by Mainbocher in Paris to meet any head of state; but, for sightseeing tours in the heat of August, I'd gone to a children's shop and bought a cheap cotton dress and a pair of Mary Jane pumps with a strap across the instep. However, I left off sightseeing every afternoon and gussied up to impress *Il Duce*.

Day after day, the phone rang on the dot of five and Lady Jones reported, "His Excellency is tied up today. I'll phone you about the situation tomorrow." This went on until one sweltering afternoon when I took a chance on once more being stood up by Mussolini and failed to change. Of course that was the day Lady Jones phoned to say, "His Excellency has just sent his motor to fetch you. It should be at the hotel by now!" There was nothing to

At Rome, in 1927, Mussolini gave a party.

A Anita Loos con
simpatia

Mussolini

Roma giugno 1927 - V

do but meet the dictator in the rumpled cotton dress of a Roman child.

The Great Man's car turned out to be a rather battered taxi; its driver proudly informed me that *Il Duce* didn't own an automobile but merely hired that taxi by the day.

Lady Jones met me at the entrance of the Palazzo Venezia and led me to *Il Duce*'s office. It proved to be a dark and cavernous room, so long that it required a nerve-wracking walk to reach the Great Man. He stood under a light-trough that extended the full length of his desk and served to illuminate him in a blaze of glory.

When Her Ladyship introduced me, the expression on *Il Duce*'s face was reminiscent of that with which D.W. Griffith had greeted me so many years ago. Looking me over, *Il Duce* exclaimed to Mrs. Jones, "But she's a bambina!"

Lady Jones placed me in a chair facing Mussolini, where I sat throughout the entire interview while he paced back and forth, keeping well within the illumination provided by that trough. I had a feeling that *Il Duce* gave a performance for anybody anywhere. He was always "on."

Mussolini's Italian conversation with Lady Jones led me to think she'd told him I was a serious journalist whom it would be to his advantage to impress; I never heard her mention a new book called *I Signori Preferiscono Le Bionde*.

I'm equally certain *Il Duce* thought I was going to ask him bitchy female questions, because he never stopped questioning *me*. He seemed interested in Douglas Fairbanks, and it crossed my mind that he and Doug were spiritual brothers. Only when *Il Duce* finally ran out of breath did I feel it incumbent to speak out to ask, "Will Your Excellency ever visit the United States?" Her Ladyship translated the question, at which *Il Duce* popped his eyes in the best Mussolini manner, banged the desk with that famous fist of iron, and declared, "*I am chained to this desk!*"

Lady Jones then signaled that the interview was over, and produced a photograph for Mussolini to dedicate. He wrote, "*A Anita Loos con simpatia*." It is difficult to translate "*simpatia*"; its connotation doesn't exist in our language. It suggests "camaraderie" and means, in effect, "You and I understand each other."

That Lady Jones was as insincere as her boss came into focus the next day when she phoned to demand a hundred dollars for having introduced me to Mussolini. Suddenly remembering Wilson Mizner's response in a like situation, I told her I was in the market to sell the introduction back to her at half the price; at which she slammed down the receiver and gave up.

So, of those three smart cookies who met that day in *Il Duce*'s office, I was to come out the winner. Mussolini's attempt to rip off his country failed, as did Lady Jones' more modest rip-off of me. But I had the advantage of having been schooled by Wilson Mizner.

4

GENTLEMEN PREFER BLONDES

This caricature by Ralph Barton is a figment of the artist's imagination. I never learned to type, having always found it more cosy to loll on a chaise longue and write on a clipboard. Just the same, Ralph's cartoon suggests a certain moment when Fate edged up and nudged me with its elbow.

The event actually took place when I was en route from New York to Hollywood with Douglas Fairbanks Senior. In the carefree days of silent films, Doug traveled with an exuberant group. In addition to me and my husband, who directed the films I wrote for Doug, there was an assistant director, two sparring partners, a masseur, a publicity staff, and assorted "yes men." And accompanying us on that jaunt was a Broadway cutie who was being imported to Hollywood for a screen test.

That girl was a lot bigger than I was, but she was being waited on by every male in our troupe. If she happened to drop the magazine she was reading, several of them would jump to retrieve it, whereas I was allowed to tug heavy suitcases from their racks while those same men failed to note my efforts.

That girl and I were both in the pristine years of early youth; we shared about the same degree of comeliness, and mine was less contrived, for she was a quite unnatural blonde. Concerning our mental acumen, there was nothing to discuss; I was the smarter. But there was some mystifying difference between us. Why did she so far outdistance me in feminine allure? Could her power, like that of Samson, have something to do with her hair?

Now, I wasn't annoyed over my husband's attentions to that budding starlet. I had long ceased expecting gallantry from a spouse who took my services for granted. His dependence on me had become a sort of joke that everybody enjoyed, myself included. One of a few laughs Sam Goldwyn gave us that was not a boo-boo had been when he remarked with a chuckle, "Emerson is one of them guys that lives by the sweat of his *frau.*" And the nephew of Marion Davies, my adored pal Charlie Lederer, had paraphrased a song-title by dubbing my husband "Sweet Mister E. of Life."

As the train sped on its way I began to harbor a resentment of blondes that cut quite deeply, and presently I singled out a stupid creature who had bedazzled one of America's foremost intellects, H.L. Mencken.

Now the long crush I'd had on H.L. had had a frustrating response. Not that Menck wasn't fond of me; I was even included in his inner circle of male friends. I sometimes caused Menck to laugh, but in the matter of sentiment he preferred a witless blonde. The situation was palpably unjust.

I thought it over as our train raced across the plains of Kansas, until in a spirit of malice I said to myself, "I'll fix *her!*" So I reached for one of my large yellow pads and began to write down my thoughts, not bitterly, as I might have done had I been a real novelist, but with an amusement that was a hangover from childhood, when one tends to look on grownups as figures of fun. (A certain friend used to compare my slant on life to that of a ten-year-old, chortling with glee over some disaster.)

The plot of *Gentlemen Prefer Blondes,* on examination, is almost as tragic as a novel by Feodor Dostoevski. This was recognized when the Soviet authorities allowed my book to be translated into Russian and even hailed it as evidence of the exploitation of blondes by predatory magnates of the capitalistic system. With their fondness for grief, the Russians stripped *G.P.B.* of fun and uncovered a plot that concerned the rape of its teenage heroine; her attempt to murder the culprit, unsuccessful only because she is clumsy with a gun; her flight into the gangster-infested New York of Prohibition days; her pursuit by males, most of whom try to pay her off at bargain rates; and her final engulfment in the grim monotony of Philadelphia, from which she escapes into Hollywood stardom, financed by an idiotic husband.

With such material, a novelist like Sherwood Anderson, Theodore Dreiser, William Faulkner, or Ernest Hemingway would have curdled his readers' blood with massive indignation. Scott Fitzgerald would have shed bittersweet tears over such eventualities. But I could only look on such human behavior as funny.

74

This adoring pose is only a put-on. My mind was on somebody else.

a.

The Prince of Wales is wonderful — even if he were not a prince he ~~would~~ make his living playing the ukelele if he had a little more practice.

b.

I decided I would write down everything he said to me in my diary so I would always have it and I could go back and read it over and over ~~find~~ when I'm really old so I asked him if he had fallen off his horse lately and he said he had not.

c.

"I don't care what you do, gentlemen — I'm going to smoke a cigar."

d.

L. likes the French much better than the English as the French tarts she meets are all making good hauls out of men — whereas the English aristocracy are doing it for their own amusement and doing many a good tart out of a job.

e.

It was really when I shot Mr. Jennings that I really got the idea to go in the movies (cinema)

f.

I mean French is really very easy because their words are really a great deal alike I mean because rou means a street and roué means a gentleman Also they use the word shriek for everything while we only use it for gentlemen who resemble Rudolf Valentino

Outfitted for traveling, I left for Europe, taking a notebook along to jot down my observations.

I finished a short description of Menck's "loved one" as our train was nearing Hollywood; it was time to pack up and get back to writing frenetic screenplays for Doug Fairbanks, so I stuck the manuscript into the flap of a suitcase and, for six months or more, forgot all about it.

I might never have thought of it again, for I was a movie writer and wouldn't have dreamed that my heroine had any place on celluloid. But later, back in New York, I ran across the smudged pages of my little critique and mailed it to Menck in Baltimore, to give him a laugh at his own expense (this being several blondes later than the one who had inspired me).

Menck enjoyed my joke; and, although it hit close to home, he suggested that the sketch be published. He had just sold out his interest in *Smart Set*, where he would gladly have printed my treatise, and he was diffident about the *American Mercury*, which he now edited. "Young lady," he warned me, "you're the first American writer ever to make fun of sex!" He then suggested that I send the article to *Harper's Bazaar*, where "it'll be lost among the ads and won't offend the *boobus americanus*."

The editor of *Harper's Bazaar* was Henry Sell, and he approved my piece. "But you've started your heroine on a tour of Europe," said Henry. "Why don't you let her continue?"

The assignment was easy, as I was about to tour Europe myself. So I continued Lorelei's adventures and sent

each month's installment back by mail.

The image of Menck remained ever in my mind. I chose Arkansas as my heroine's birthplace because of the essay Menck had written in which he branded Arkansas as "the Sahara of the Bozarts." And, as a crowning insult to the blonde of Mencken's choice, I made her a native of Little Rock.

Now *Harper's Bazaar* was a ladies' publication, but by the time the third chapter of *Gentlemen Prefer Blondes* appeared, gentlemen were beginning to read about her. Advertisements for men's apparel, cigars, whisky, and sporting-goods began pouring into the magazine; newsstand sales doubled, tripled, then quadrupled.

After Lorelei's story ended in the *Bazaar*, sex as usual became an issue in my life: a beau of mine, Tom Smith, was on the staff of the Liveright publishing house, and he asked if I'd like to have a few copies of my story in book form to give friends at Christmas. I thought it a good idea, whereupon Tom caused his firm to print a small "vanity" edition of fifteen hundred copies. (Which accounts for the fact that those few copies have become collectors' items.)

The first edition of *Gentlemen Prefer Blondes* sold out the same day it reached the bookshops. And, although the second edition numbered sixty-five thousand copies, it was exhausted almost as quickly.

Stokie had indeed spoken with a sort of E.S.P. when he said that I and my girl

friends were rather a peculiar breed.

Ralph Barton drew the illustrations for *Gentlemen Prefer Blondes*. He had been hired as a cartoonist by Henry Sell, the editor of *Harper's Bazaar*, but after putting him on salary, Sell had to dig up subjects for Ralph to caricature. And when the first segment of my book came into Sell's hands, he immediately saw it as material for Ralph to illustrate. Ralph did so with gusto, during which he naturally ascribed the success of my story to his illustrations. But when the

"Dr. Froyd seemed to think that I was quite a famous case."

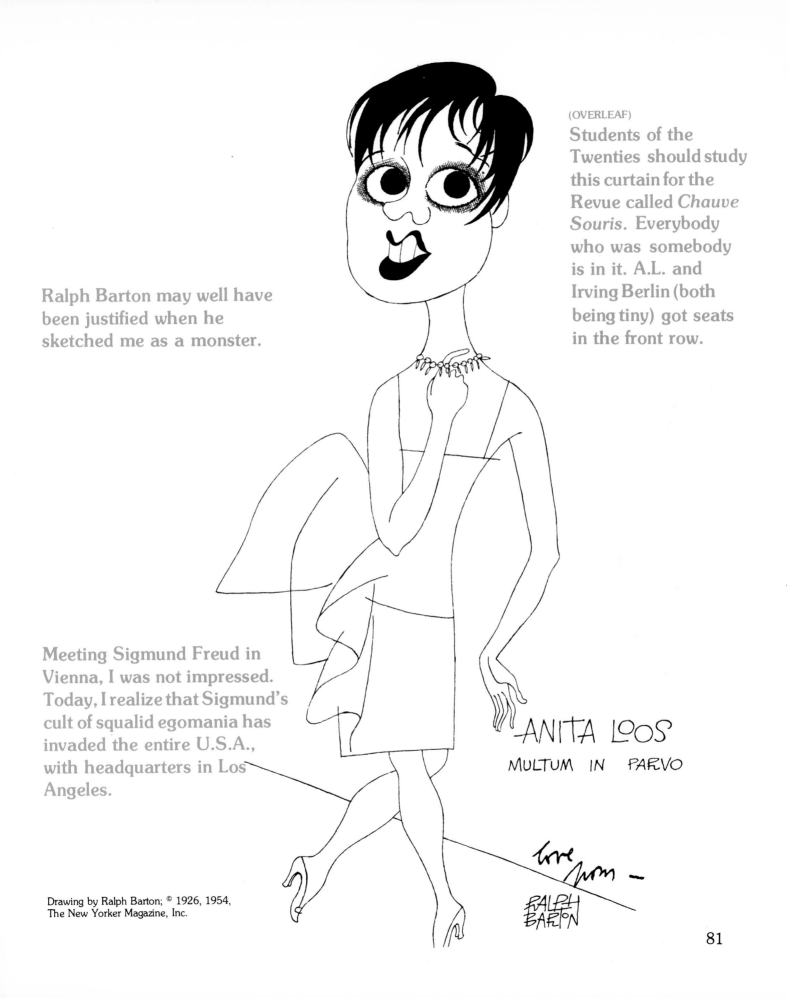

Ralph Barton may well have been justified when he sketched me as a monster.

(OVERLEAF) Students of the Twenties should study this curtain for the Revue called *Chauve Souris*. Everybody who was somebody is in it. A.L. and Irving Berlin (both being tiny) got seats in the front row.

Meeting Sigmund Freud in Vienna, I was not impressed. Today, I realize that Sigmund's cult of squalid egomania has invaded the entire U.S.A., with headquarters in Los Angeles.

ANITA LOOS
MULTUM IN PARVO

love from —
RALPH BARTON

FIRST ROW—from left to right
    AL JOLSON
    JOHN EMERSON
    ANITA LOOS
    IRVING BERLIN
    DAVID BELASCO
    LENORE ULRIC
    JOHN BARRYMORE
    MICHAEL STRANGE

SECOND ROW—from left to right
    ANNA PAVLOWA
    JOSEF HOFMAN
    REINA BELASCO GEST
    JOHN DREW
    THEODORE ROOSEVELT
    MARIE JERITZA
    GIULIO GATTI-CASAZZA
    GERALDINE FARRAR
    MARY GARDEN

THIRD ROW—from left to right
    ELSIE DE WOLFE
    ARTHUR BRISBANE
    MRS. WM. RANDOLPH HEARST
    HENRY BLACKMAN SELL
    CONDE NAST
    IRENE CASTLE
    FRANK CROWINSHIELD
    MRS. H. PAYNE WHITNEY
    KENNETH MACGOWAN
    ALAN DALE
    RAY LONG

FOURTH ROW—from left to right
    SAM BERNARD
    MARILYN MILLER
    ED WYNN
    MRS. J. BORDEN HARRIMAN
    CHARLES DANA GIBSON
    ALEXANDER WOOLLCOTT
    MRS. LYDIG HOYT
    FRANKLIN P. ADAMS
    NEYSA McMEIN
    HEYWOOD BROUN
    DORIS KEANE
    PERCY HAMMOND

FIFTH ROW—from left to right
    MORANZONI
    ANN MORGAN
    BURNS MANTLE
    MRS. W. K. VANDERBILT
    WILLARD HUNTINGTON WRIGHT
    S. JAY KAUFMAN
    HERBERT SWOPE
    WALTER CATLETT
    SOPHIE BRASLAU
    DOROTHY GISH
    DAVID W. GRIFFITH
    LILLIAN GISH
    ELIZABETH MARBURY
    LEON ERROL
    ZOE AKINS

LOWER RIGHT BOX—from left to right
    FYODOR CHALIAPIN
    LUCREZIA BORI
    MADAME ALDA

LEFT UPPER BOX—from left to right
    MAUDE ADAMS
    JOHN McCORMACK
    CHARLES CHAPLIN
    MARECHAL JOFFRE

RIGHT UPPER BOX—from left to right
    LAURETTE TAYLOR
    FRANCES STARR
    CLARE SHERIDAN
    HARTLEY MANNERS

82

THE CURTAIN BETWEEN THE ACTS

FOYER S. R. O.—from left to right
- A. D. LASKER
- SAMUEL L. ROTHAPFEL
- NICHOLAS MURRAY BUTLER
- RALPH BARTON
- JESSE LASKY
- EDWARD ZIEGLER
- WILLIAM GUARD
- LOUIS UNTERMEYER
- J. J. SHUBERT
- LEE SHUBERT
- F. RAY COMSTOCK
- MORRIS GEST
- OLIVER M. SAYLER
- BORIS ANISFELD
- ROBERT EDMOND JONES
- RING LARDNER
- STEPHEN RATHBUN
- ARMAND VECSZY
- ANDREAS DE SEGUROLA
- PAPI
- RAYMOND HITCHCOCK

SIXTH ROW—from left to right
- ADOLF ZUKOR
- ROBERT G. WELSH
- FAY BAINTER
- LAWRENCE REAMER
- GERTRUDE HOFFMAN
- WALTER DAMROSCH
- MARY NASH
- WILHELM MENGELBERG
- CHARLES DARNTON
- OTTO H. KAHN
- FRANK A. MUNSEY
- FLO ZIEGFELD
- ARTURO BODANZKY
- ADOLPH OCHS
- JOHN RUMSEY

SEVENTH ROW—from left to right
- LUDWIG LEWISOHN
- GEORGE S. KAUFMAN
- LYNN FONTANNE
- MARC CONNELLY
- GEO. M. COHAN
- JOHN MacMAHON
- HENRY KREHBIEL
- MRS. ENRICO CARUSO
- BEN-AMI
- DOROTHY DALTON
- DAVID WARFIELD
- ROBERT C. BENCHLEY

EIGHTH ROW—from left to right
- KARL KITCHEN
- ANTONIO SCOTTI
- FANNY HURST
- HUGO RIESENFELD
- VERA FOKINA
- MICHEL FOKINE
- AVERY HOPWOOD
- CONSTANCE TALMADGE
- ANNA FITZIU
- REGINALD VANDERBILT
- DR. FRANK CRANE
- YASHA HEIFETZ

NINTH ROW—from left to right
- EUGENE O'NEILL
- PROF. ROERICH
- JOSEPH URBAN
- ARTHUR HORNBLOW, Jr.
- PAUL MEYER
- ELSIE JANIS
- PAUL BLOCK
- JOHN FARRAR
- SERGEI RACHMANINOFF
- HERBERT HOOVER
- JOHN GOLDEN
- WINCHELL SMITH
- JAY GOULD

CHAUVE-SOURIS—BY RALPH BARTON

©UNDERWOOD & UNDERWOOD
STUDIOS, N. Y.

After Ralph Barton married Carlotta
Monterey he came to hate her. She
later divorced him to marry Eugene
O'Neill. Ralph committed suicide
leaving a very curious farewell letter.

Ralph Barton's Last Essay to Which He Gave the Title:

OBIT

Every one who has known me and who hears of this
will have a different hypothesis to offer to
explain why I did it. Practically all of these
hypotheses will be dramatic and completely wrong.
Any sane doctor knows the reasons for a suicide
are invariably psychopathic and the true suicide
type manufactures his own difficulties.

I have had few real difficulties. I have had on
the contrary an exceptionally glamorous life as
life goes and have had more than my share of
appreciation and affection. The most charming,
intelligent and important people I have known,
and they liked me, and the list of my enemies
is very flattering to me.

I have always had excellent health, but from
childhood I have suffered from melancholia,
which in the past few years has begun to show
definite symptoms of depressive insanity. It
has prevented my getting anywhere like the
full value out of my talent and for the past
three years has made work a torture to do at all.

It has made it impossible for me to enjoy the
simple pleasures of life that seem to get other
people through.

I have run from wife to wife, from house to house,
and from country to country, a ridiculous effort
to escape from myself. In doing so I am very much
afraid that I have wrought a great deal of un-
happiness to those who have loved me.

In particular, my remorse is bitter over my
failure to appreciate my beautiful lost angel,
Carlotta -- the only woman I ever loved and
who I respect and admire above all the rest of
the human race. She is the one person who could
have saved me, had I been savable.

She did her best.

No one ever had a more devoted or more understanding
wife.

I do hope she will understand what my malady
was and forgive me a little.

No one thing is responsible for this and no
one person except myself.

If the gossips insist on something more definite
and thrilling as a reason, let them choose my
pending appointment with my dentist or the fact
that I happen to be painfully short of cash at
the moment. No other single reason is more
important or less temporary. After all, one has
to choose a moment and the air is full of reasons
at any given moment.

I've done it because I'm fed up with inventing
devices for getting through twenty-four hours
every day and with bridging over a few months
periodically with some purely artificial interest,
such as a new 'gal' who annoys me to the point
where I forget my own troubles.

I present the remains with compliments to any
medical school that fancies them, or soap to be
made of them. In them I have not the slightest
interest, except that I want them to cause as
little bother as possible.

I kiss my dear children -- and Carlotta.

85

Tauchnitz edition came out in paperback without any pictures, it was just as huge a success. So Ralph took his revenge on me and drew a picture featuring everything that's hateful and malicious in my nature.

Ralph's viewpoint had merit. I've always thought there's something rather monstrous about any female who writes.

There were many beauties in Ralph's life; one of them was Carlotta Monterey who, after divorcing him, married America's great playwright, Eugene O'Neill. Ralph had been notoriously unfaithful to Carlotta, and soon after his divorce he married the brilliant French composer Germaine Tailleferre, the one woman member of an avant garde musical group in Paris called "Les Six."

But when Carlotta became Mrs. Eugene O'Neill, Ralph, berserk with jealousy, committed suicide. Carlotta had married a man who was more famous than he.

The success of the book, *Gentlemen Prefer Blondes*, was followed by a stage production that toured the country before opening in New York at the Times Square Theater on September 28, 1926. It was produced by Edgar Selwyn, and starred June Walker as Lorelei, Edna Hibbard as Dorothy, and Frank Morgan as Henry Spofford. It ran for six months which, in those days, was considered lengthy, so the excitement surrounding my little story continued.

There was the usual competition in Hollywood for the movie-rights to a

best-seller, and Paramount won out. The price paid for movie-rights was as colossal in those days as now. I've forgotten the exact figure, but movie money is like Hollywood spangles; it has a tendency to drop off and get lost.

The first movie version of *G.P.B.* was directed by Mal St. Clair. It was nearing the end of silent pictures, and Mal insisted on filming one single scene with sound. So, right in the middle of its silent footage, the voices of Lorelei and her girlfriend Dorothy were abruptly heard. The scene showed the two girls at Prunier's, the famous fish restaurant in Paris, where, not knowing French, they speculate about the meaning of the word "poisson" on the menu and—thinking it a French equivalent for "poison"—begin to lose their appetites.

In 1948, the Broadway producers, Herman Levin and Oliver Smith, came up with an idea of setting *G.P.B* to music. One of their production meetings was held in the living-room of our director, John C. Wilson. And, for some reason I don't remember, the painter Marcel Vertès happened to sketch our session.

In the right foreground of his sketch is the Wilsons' dachshund, Fan Tan. But because Natasha Wilson was a Romanov princess, she'd given her pet the aristocratic nickname of "Poopooni."

To the left of Poopooni is Jack Wilson. He had previously produced most of Noel Coward's comedies, had directed *Present Laughter,* and was geared to put the most exquisite taste into a show

86

Jesse Lasky outbid every other studio and captured *G.P.B.* for Paramount. Then followed the usual search among young Hollywood actresses for a blonde. We chose Ruth Taylor who was so ideal that she took the role seriously, married a millionaire as soon as the picture was completed, and has never acted again.

Marcel Vertès sketched a production conference for the
for the musical version of *Gentlemen Prefer Blondes*.

that was basically rowdy.

I can't recall the owner of the stunning back at Jack's left. She must have been there on the invitation of our producer. Wherever Herman is, there's bound to be a dishy female.

Natasha Wilson comes next, and today neither she nor I can figure out how she got into this picture. Natasha, born a Romanov princess, became involved in the theater through her very happy marriage to Jack, but she hated the theater, and branded show-biz as her own private version of "The Curse of the Romanovs." It's probable that Vertès pulled her in and forced her to pose because she is so pretty.

Oliver Smith's long frame is draped over Natasha's couch. Oliver's décor turned the gaudy milieu of *G.P.B.* into a work of art. And, because as producer he had to pay for the sets, Oliver's price was right.

Authoress A. Loos, recently returned from Paris, here sports a hat from Balenciaga.

Bending over Jule Styne, who had just come through with our musical score, is the as yet unknown Carol Channing.

Next in view is Herman, the producer of any author's dreams. He lures the top talents in every field, turns the job over to them, promptly gets lost in a poker game, and never thinks of butting in.

If one believed the papparazzi, the author was supposed to pick out her blonde.

Mal was inspired to sketch the authoress.

The author of that silent film, with blonde Ruth Taylor, brunette Alice White, and our director Mal St. Clair.

At Herman's right is Miles White, whose costume designs won the Tony Award for *Gentlemen Prefer Blondes.*

Last, and by all means least of this talented group, is Joe Fields, whose book for *G.P.B.* was so inept it had to be pitched out. Joe replaced our sex story with one that concerned bootlegging in the Twenties, and was full of characters running around with violin cases that contained sawed-off shotguns. He even went so far as to change the names of the two leading characters to Mabel and Geraldine. When Joe's script was read by his sister, the fine lyricist Dorothy Fields, she called me up and said, "Nita, you can't let Joe do this to you." So the script was rewritten practically on the cuff by A. Loos.

(Missing from Vertès' sketch is the lyricist Leo Robin. It was he who coined that stirring aphorism that sums up Lorelei's lifestyle: "Diamonds Are a Girl's Best Friend.")

The chorus line Herman assembled for *G.P.B.* was the result of his masterly womanizing. For Herman was, and is, the last of the lusty Broadway producers. Most of today's breed get bogged down fighting labor unions. Considering themselves a branch of Western Union, they devote their efforts to the delivery of messages. In the instance of Hal Prince and Stephen Sondheim, they remind me of the old Algonquin Round Table. A recent offbeat musical produced to show their erudition brought forth a trenchant remark that the character they'd be most capable of

93

handling would be Narcissus. At any rate, their one-dimensional pessimism reminds me of that quote that states, "Americans have become decadent before they achieved culture."

Also, in these days, some producers are intent on proving that the majority of gentlemen prefer gentlemen. But Herman Levin is normally dazzled by the ladies and chooses his chorus well. Among these showgirls, one of them, Greg Sherwood, married Horace Dodge (of the Detroit Dodges) and is today the doyenne of Palm Beach society.

Alice White as Dorothy was bolstered by Ford Sterling, who was borrowed from the Keystone Kops for the silent film version of *G.P.B.*

The adorable British comedian, G. P. Huntley, imported from London for the role of Sir Francis Beekman had to suffer the pangs of Prohibition. But he managed to remain agreeably tight on Wild Cherry Cough Syrup and Lydia Pinkham's Vegetable Compound.

Ruth Taylor's hair looks dark, but that's the fault of the camera. She was a glorious natural blonde.

679-2/11

TIME

THE WEEKLY NEWSMAGAZINE

Boris Cho

CAROL CHANNING

"It has to be serious or it won't be funny."

96

Carol and I still laugh over this disdainful pose.

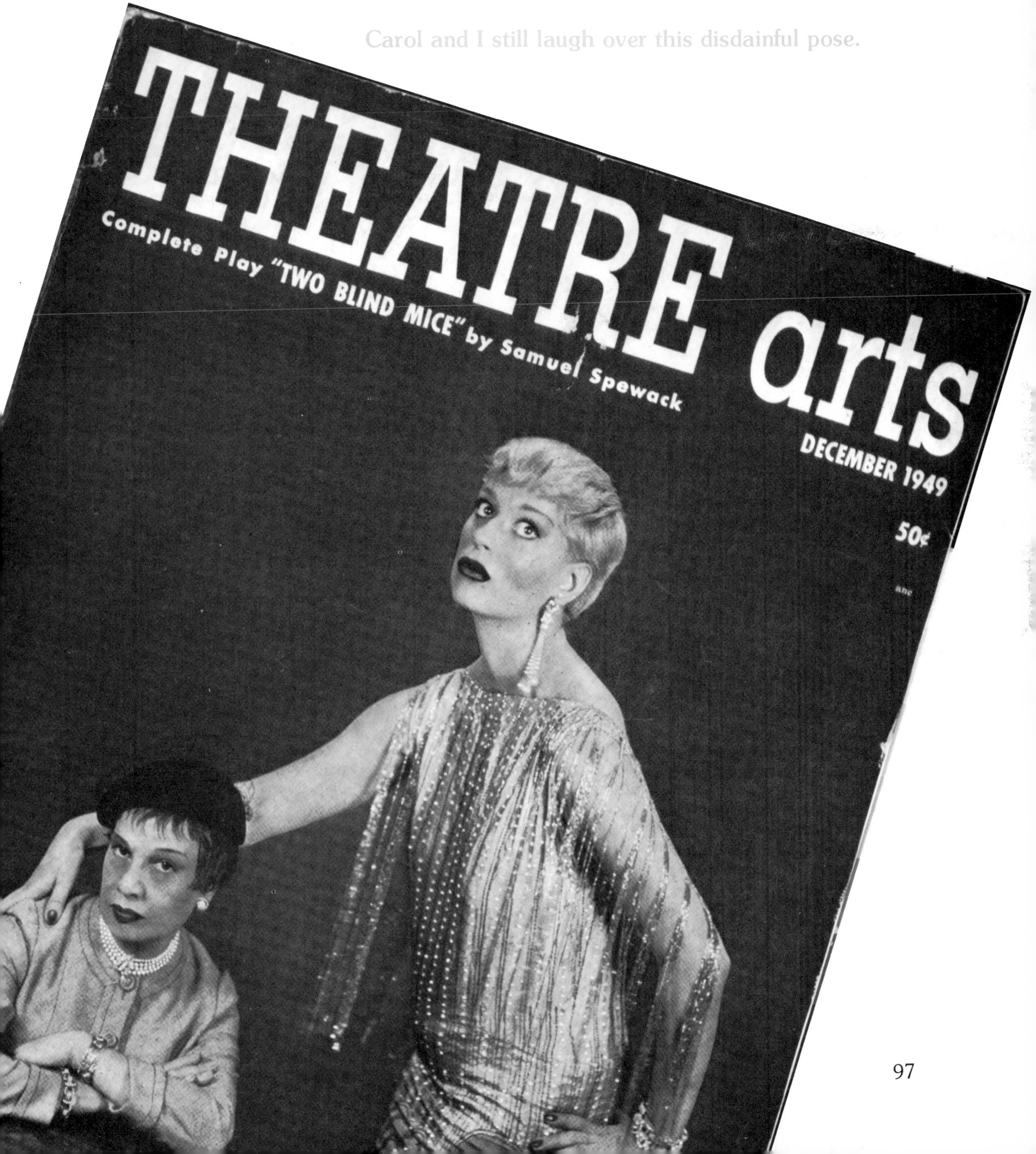

THEATRE arts

Complete Play "TWO BLIND MICE" by Samuel Spewack

DECEMBER 1949

50¢

97

New Musical in Manhattan

Gentlemen Prefer Blondes (book by Joseph Fields & Anita Loos; music by Jule Styne; lyrics by Leo Robin) lets the famous Lorelei Lee of the '20s gold-dig once more—this time to music. The blonde is played by Carol Channing, who last season rocketed from nowhere to minor fame in *Lend an Ear*. Last week she drew rave reviews; one critic ecstatically called her "the funniest female since Fanny Brice and Beatrice Lillie."

That Comedienne Channing is now heading a smash hit there can be little doubt; nevertheless, she is often the sole support of an ailing show. Where *Blondes* gets hold of a good thing, it suffers from Lorelei's belief that you can't have too much of it; even without a good thing, it follows the same general line.

Strapping (5 ft. 9 in.) Actress Channing herself represents a triumph of miscasting. She can be a very funny female indeed, but in *Blondes* she suggests the football-playing "heroine" of a varsity show more than the deceptively fragile Lorelei. With her tremendous saucer eyes, her exaggerated mincing gait, her voice that goes suddenly Dixie and suddenly husky, and her simultaneous suggestion that butter wouldn't melt in her mouth and steel bars would bend in her hands, she is not so much a broad caricature as a pure original. She is forced to overdo the whole thing, but in such individual numbers as *A Little Girl from Little Rock* it richly pays off.

While Actress Channing is a happily blown-up Lorelei, the script is a sadly watered-down *Blondes*; and the score is almost everywhere commonplace. Lorelei's less rapacious pal Dorothy (Yvonne Adair), after having all the life knocked out of her in the script, takes up a lot of dull romantic room in the show. And Dancer Anita Alvarez, who is always good for an eccentric specialty or two, is foolishly converted into a stand-by.

Thanks to Comedienne Channing's song numbers and to some fast, youthful Agnes de Mille dance routines, the show achieves an air of liveliness in places. What it never achieves is any real feeling of the '20s, or the right nostalgia for them.

There can never be too many Carol Channings.

These costumes designed by Miles
White featured a martini, complete
with cherry.

NOTHING TO DISCUSS=
JULE STYNE=

PREFER YOU=

:LELAND=

...WILL BE TERRIFIC=

TEX AND JINX=

WESTERN
UNION

CONGRATULA
by WESTERN UN

N34CC 2R PD

SI NEWYORK NY 627P DEC 8 1949

ANITA LOOS

ZIEGFELD THEATRE NYK

GOOD LUCK AND BEST WISHES

VINCENT SARDI JR

WESTERN
UNION

D150CC 7A PD

WUX NEW YORK NY 707P DEC 8 1949

MISS ANITA LOOS ZIEGFELD THEATRE

BACK STAGE 54 ST AND 6 AVE NYK

BEST WISHES FOR A GREAT SUCCESS AND OUR FONDEST

ROUBEN AND

Mamoulian

WESTERN
UNION

E72CC 4R PD

CP NEWYORK NY 521P DEC 8 1949

MISS ANITA LOOS

BACKSTAGE ZIEGFELD THEATRE NYK

I PREFER YOU. LOVE

BILLY ROSE

750P

WESTERN
UNION

NBC15 PD=NRP NEWYORK NY 8 411P=   1949 DEC 8 PM 4 40

ANITA LOOS, ZIEGFELD THEATRE

SIXTH AVE AND 54 ST=

DEAR ANITA MY LOVE TO YOU AND AN ENORMOUS SUCCESS TONIGHT=

NOEL=

WESTERN
UNION

E54CC 1F NL PD

NEW YORK NY DEC 7 1949

MISS ANITA LOOS, ZIEGFELD THEATRE

54 ST AND 6 AVE NYK

BUT DARLING WE NOT ONLY PREFER BUT WE LOVE YOU

AND ALWAYS

MARY MARTIN AND RICHARD HALLIDAY

1255P

WESTERN
UNION

NA519 DL PD VIA AR (R

MISS ANITA LOOS:

=FAIRFAX HOTEL 116 E

:ALREADY WE HEAR BY THE

PREFER BLONDES AND THEY

AS IN PHILADELPHIA. CONG

FRANCE AND EDGAR=

Edgar Ber

WESTERN
UNION

NA980 PD=NEWYORK NY 8 1010P=

=ANITA LOOS=ZIEGFELD THEATRE=

WISHES=

:GISHES=

WESTERN
UNION

*BB159

B=NVA958 PD=NEWHAVEN CONN 7 942P=

MISS ANITA LOOS=

DLR AM ZIEGFIELD THEATRE AVENUE OF THE AMERICAS NYK=

...LL BE THINKING OF YOU WITH ALL   MY HEART=

:KATE HEPBURN=

CONGRA
by WEST

...)=WUX TDL CULV...

...OOS=

...EGFELD THEATR...

...T WISHES FOR...

LOVE...

GEORGE CUKOR=..

WESTERN
UNION

NA249 PD=NWF NEWYORK NY 8 151P=

ANITA LOOS=

FAIRFAX HOTEL 116 EAST 56 ST=

MAY YOU REEK WITH SUCCESS= LOVE=

COLE=

WESTERN
UNION

NA555 PD=NEW YORK NY 8 413P=

MISS ANITA LOOS=

:ZIEGFELD THEA=

:DEAR ANITA YOU HAVE CREATED A GREAT G

MUSICAL AND I REJOICE IN THE SUCCESS I

GOING TO HAVE WITH LOVE FROM=

:DOUGLAS= *Pollard*

CONGRATULATIO
by WESTERN UNION

NB255 PD=RK NEWYORK NY 8 632P=

:ANITA LOOS, ZIEGFELD THEATRE=

:GLAD TO GET YOU OUT OF PHILADELPHIA AND HOPE YOU

FOREVER=

RICHARD RODGERS AND OSCAR HAMMERSTEIN 2ND=.

CONGRAT
by WESTE

L7CC 6L CGN PD

NEWYORK NY 555P D

ANITA LOOS,

ZIEGFELD THEATRE,

CHEERS AND BRAVOS FOR YOUR IMMO

AGNES DE MILLE=

750P

LOVE GOOD LUCK AND LOTS OF DIAMONDS

MADELINE BOB SHERWOOD

WESTERN UNION (48)..

JOSEPH L. EGAN
PRESIDENT

BAO 76

B. NVA930 PD=C NEWHAVEN CONN 8 637P=

ANITA LOOS=

GENTLEMEN PREFER BLONDES CO ZIEGFIELD THEATRE NYK=

DEAR ANITA: I AM SO VERY VERY HAPPY FOR YOU. LOVE=
IRENE SELZNICK

CONGRATULATIONS
by WESTERN UNION

NEW YORK NY 540P DEC 8 1949

D145CC 7A PD

MISS ANITA LOOS ZIEGFIELD THEATRE

54 ST AND 6 AVE NYK

YOU KNOW WHAT I WISH LOVE

ELEANOR HOLM ROSE   750P

CONGRATULATIONS
by WESTERN UNION

1949 DEC 8 PM 9 15

NB444 PD=ASHEVILLE NCAR 8 705P=

MISS ANITA LOOS=ZIEGFIELD THEATRE=

HONEY CHILE YOU ALL JUST DOWN RIGHT INTEGRIN LOVE=
TALLUULAAH=

CONGRATULATIONS
UNION

NA232 CGN PD=NEWYORK NY 8 250P=

ANITA LOOS=

ZIEGFIELD THEATRE=

DEAR ANITA, HAPPY FOR YOUR GREAT SUCCESS GLAD TO KNOW
GENTLEMN PREFER BLONDES DOING IT TO MUSIC THIS SEASON LOVE=
MAE WEST=

WESTERN UNION (53)

W. P. MARSHALL, PRESIDENT

NA111 PD VIA AR NFU= NWF NEWYORK NY DEC 8 1157P=

ANITA LOOS=FAIRFAX HOTEL=

HAVE BEEN THINKING OF YOU ALL EVENING
BREAK ALL RECORDS ON BROADWAY

IRENE

We stayed awake all night reading telegrams.

LIFE

MARILYN MONROE
AND JANE RUSSELL
IN
'GENTLEMEN PREFER BLONDES'

MOVIES

20 CENTS
MAY 25, 1953

MARILYN TAKES OVER AS LORELEI

She is the latest in long line of diamond-grabbers

Lorelei Lee is harvesting diamonds again. Veteran of a novel by Anita Loos (1925), a play (1926), a silent movie (1928), a musical comedy (1949), she is now in a stupendous Technicolor talkie of *Gentlemen Prefer Blondes*. She is played by Marilyn Monroe, who is the least ingenuous of the Lorelei line but yields to none in cheerful rapacity.

In the new 20th Century-Fox version Marilyn sings and dances with a surprising technical competence. Full-fleshed and fancy-free, she and her dark-haired girl friend, played by Jane Russell, start the show off with a bang in tight red dresses (*see cover*) for the song *The Little Girl from Little Rock*. They go racing on through a broad-comedy modern-dress version of the old plot as Lorelei stuffs her pocketbook with cash and bedecks her person with trinkets offered to her by gullible millionaires. In her biggest number she spurns a whole panel of penniless and prostrate admirers (*left*) and gives their fallen forms the benefit of her philosophy of life: *Diamonds Are a Girl's Best Friend.*

It is customary for authors to deride film versions of their works. But Charlie Lederer's script for *G.P.B.* was better than I could have written myself. As for the casting of Lorelei, Marilyn was more authentic but Carol was funnier.

DORA BRYAN
in GENTLEMEN PREFER BLONDES

KENNETH WAGG, & ADDEY, OWEN & HOLLERITH LTD., PRESENT

DORA BRYAN
in
GENTLEMEN PREFER
BLONDES

Book by
JOSEPH FIELDS & ANITA LOOS
Adapted from the novel by ANITA LOOS

Music by
JULE STYNE · LE

GUY   DONALD   ANNE   RO
MIDDLETON   STEWART   HART   PAL

VALERIE   MICHAEL   TOTT
WALSH   MALNICK   TRUMAN

Diamanter det er det, der dur
&
En lille en fra Little Rock

Fra operetten

GENTLEMEN
FORETRÆKKER
BLONDINER

Efter ANITA LOOS' berømte bog

MUSIK:
JULE STYNE

ENGELSKE TEKSTER:
LEO ROBIN

DANSKE TEKSTER:
ARVID MÜLLER

MØRKS MUSIKFORLAG
KØBENHAVN

HIT SONGS
EXCLUSIVE!
MAY
FPI 15c

Song Hits
MAGAZINE

CORRECT LYRICS BY PERMISSION OF COPYRIGHT OWNERS

SONG HITS of Tomorrow

SONG HITS of Today

Feature Story By
DINAH SHORE

STAY WELL

THERE'S NO TOMORROW

DADDY'S LITTLE GIRL

LILY OF LAGUNA

BIBBIDI-BOBBIDI-BOO

DEAR HEARTS AND
GENTLE PEOPLE

THE LITTLE GRAY
HOUSE

DIAMONDS ARE A
GIRL'S BEST FRIEND

N DREAM CAN'T I

SONG

WHY WAS I BORN

A DREAMER'S HOLIDAY

WITH MY EYES WIDE OPEN
I'M DREAMING

THE BIG MOVIE SHOW
IN THE SKY

A WONDERFUL GUY

THE OLD MASTER
PAINTER

A DREAM IS A WISH
YOUR HEART MAKES

A LITTLE GIRL
FROM LITTLE ROCK

BROKEN DOWN
MERRY-GO-ROUND

SO THIS IS LOVE

BYE BYE B

HOLLYWOO

HERMAN LEVIN and OLIVER SM
present

GENTLEME
PREFER
BLONDES

Book by JOSEPH FIELDS and ANITA LO
Music by JULE STYNE · Lyrics by LEO R
Dances and Musical Ensembles by AGNES

WITH

CAROL CHANNING · YVON
JACK McCAULEY · ERIC BRO

GEORGE S. IRVING

and the

original Broadw

Musical Direction — Milton Rosenstock · Musical Arra
Vocal Arrangements and Direction — Hug

Lorelei has been harder to kill than Rasputin.

In '31, a platinum blonde invaded my career in the guise
of a redhead. (Left to right, A.L., Jack Conway,
Lewis Stone, and Jean Harlow.)

5

M.G.M.

My long involvement with blondes was then interrupted by a redhead.

The Emersons had gone broke in the stock-market crash of '29, and I received an offer from Irving Thalberg to come out to M.G.M. to write a movie version of the naughty novel of that day, *Red Headed Woman*. My husband was more than grateful to send me back to the easy money of Hollywood, where the golden era of movies was in full swing. Although the United States was in the depths of a depression, folks were scrimping on the bare necessities of life in a search for diversion.

In 1931, it took five days on two trains to get to Hollywood, but what a deluxe five days! Because that traffic was supported by the film industry, the *Twentieth Century* to Chicago and the Santa Fe *Super Chief* to Los Angeles glittered with polished mahogany, shiny brass, and red brocade; the seats flaunted antimacassars of heavy lace. Gazing out on the flat plains of Kansas increased one's pleasure in the impeccable service and gourmet food.

On arriving at the Los Angeles station, I was given the full V.I.P. treatment by a publicity crew from M.G.M.

My conference with Irving Thalberg was scheduled for the next morning. While I was waiting to see him, I was greeted by an energetic little man who wore pince-nez glasses. On first glance, Albert Lewin (who was Thalberg's assistant) took me for an actress, and he was greatly relieved to find that I was a writer. "I'll have a chance to see you more often," he explained with what appeared to be a typical Hollywood come-on. Like most Hollywood executives, Arlie's passes were largely verbal, but we did develop a genuine friendship, and we had a lot of fun working together.

After the establishment of our romantic *entente*, Arlie escorted me into the presence of the Great Little Master. This was not my first meeting with Thalberg; I had been involved with Irving some years before, when he had been the twenty-one-year-old boy genius of Hollywood as the head of Universal.

At that time I happened to be the giggling companion of Constance Talmadge. Irving, like film fans all over the country, was wildly in love with her. His courtship, however, was beset by difficulties, for Constance was a playgirl, negligent of her own career, and unimpressed by a boyish suitor who took work seriously.

In spite of Irving's prestige as the foremost producer of the film colony, he was a rather pathetic figure. He had suffered from a heart ailment since childhood, and his natural pallor was intensified by his long working hours, shut away from the California sunshine. I was enormously touched that the shoulders of Irving's jacket were too obviously padded, in order to make him seem less boyish and more robust.

Irving Thalberg was more responsible than anyone for the Golden Age of Talkies. Who could ever blame Irving for adoring Constance Talmadge?

But it was Norma Shearer who became Mrs. Irving Thalberg.

A standing joke at the studio concerned the hours we wasted waiting for conferences with Irving. I spent time knitting this scarf. At my salary of $2,500 a week, the studio paid over $20,000 for that scarf.

He was now married to Norma Shearer, who couldn't have been more unlike Constance; haunted by ambition, Norma cared a great deal for Irving's power to create stardom. He was Pygmalion for some of the world's most fabulous Galateas; Carole Lombard, Myrna Loy, Jean Harlow, Joan Crawford, Greta Garbo, and Dolores Del Rio.

Norma was bent on marrying her boss, and Irving, preoccupied with his work, was relieved to let her make up his mind. Possibly he looked on Norma's career as a challenge, for her beauty had certain defects, among which were eyes that were small and rather close together. Irving, by expert showmanship and a judicious choice of camera angles, made a beauty and a star out of Mrs. Thalberg.

Their marriage was happy enough. Their relationship had put Irving safely in a groove of his own choice. They were both too deeply involved in their careers to take time out for love, or even fun.

When our conference got under way, Irving explained that he had prepared several scripts of *Red Headed Woman*, but his writers had only emphasized the fact that it was a rather inferior soap opera. The latest version was by Scott Fitzgerald. "But," said Irving, "Scott tried to turn the silly book into a tone-poem. So I'd like you to go ahead and make fun of its sex element."

Irving boyishly started to pace in front of his big executive desk all the while flipping a silver dollar. "Let's first of all decide about the love affair in this story," said he.

Now, *Red Headed Woman* concerned a cold-blooded schemer who was out to break up the marriage of the man for whom she worked as secretary. But her tactics were so vulgar that when he fell for them, he automatically became a nitwit. How could there possibly be a love story between such a non-hero and non-heroine?

In time, I came to learn that Thalberg looked on every film as a love story. It wasn't at all necessary for sex to be involved in the affair. Furthermore, age had nothing to do with the matter. One of Irving's most poignant romances would be *The Champ*, in which the relationship between Jackie Cooper (aged six) and Wallace Beery (a grizzly sixty) held all the rapture of a love affair. And, in *Mutiny on the Bounty*, starring Clark Gable and Charles Laughton, there would be a rivalry so bitter it could only have been based on mutual fascination. In *The Sin of Madelon Claudet*, the love affair involved an aging prostitute and her reputable, upstanding son, played by Helen Hayes and Robert Young.

Irving could spot sublimated sex in any human relationship. And he really didn't have to convince me about the deep emotional rapport that can be attained outside a bed.

At a time when most Hollywood movies dealt in contrived situations, Irving insisted that plots grow out of character. Even in the zany farces of the Marx Brothers, Irving insisted on truly human motives such as underlie the shenanigans of Molière and Feydeau and turn horseplay into art. Not that Irving carried out this system consciously. I think it would have astonished him had he lived to see that Groucho and Harpo Marx would be regarded as confrères by such men of genius as Stravinsky and Picasso.

Irving never dealt in pornography; his chief requirement in a love story was to show two sweethearts in some sort of a guileless romp with all their clothes on. Even in *Camille*, which would be graced with the steaming presence of Greta Garbo, the love scenes featured tenderness, not passion.

In concluding our conference, Irving decided I was to work alone, after which Lewin would go over each episode with me, and if he approved it, we would bring it to Irving for final criticism. I wasn't at all sure that I could make good in a new medium, but Irving assured me that Arlie Lewin would keep me straight, and I was left with the problem of glamorizing that redhead's bad behavior.

Irving's insistence on a love affair in every story posed some pretty stiff problems. One day I told him in despair, "If you *ever* make a movie of *Frankenstein*, you'll try to prove he had a mad crush on the monster he created!" "Why not?" he asked. "That old yarn is about due for a new twist."

One day as Irving paced and tossed his silver dollar, he stopped short in his tracks.

To Irving, every scenario had to be a love story, even if the sweethearts happened to be Wallace Beery and Jackie Cooper.

Garbo's Camille featured tenderness without any trace of porn

After writing a scene for *Hold Your Man* in which Jean had to sing, it transpired that her voice range covered only three notes. So Arthur Freed and Herb Nacio Brown composed a number in which Jean sang those attainable notes, and the remainder were merely hummed.

"I know what our love story can be. The heroine must be deeply in love with herself."

"I'd call that pretty unsympathetic," Arlie ventured.

"But why? The poor girl's flashy looks frighten off any man with the qualities of a hero. Who else is there for her to love, when she can only attract fools?"

Once Irving reached a conclusion, it seemed as though it should have been apparent from the beginning. And with his judgment as a guide, I completed the script in four months, which, at M.G.M. proved to be a record.

The publicity department had been busy for weeks on a competition for an actress to play that redhead. However, Irving confessed to me that the campaign was pure flimflam. He'd already decided on a certain platinum blonde who had made her first impact playing a *femme fatale* in the Howard Hughes movie *Hell's Angels*.

Irving's choice had brought forth plenty of studio opposition. He was reminded that the film critic Robert Sherwood (later to become one of America's foremost playwrights) had written, "*Hell's Angels* introduces an obstreperously alluring young lady named Jean Harlow of whom not much is likely to be heard."

On the day of Irving's first meeting with Miss Harlow, he asked me to his office to help make an appraisal of her. Jean's own tawny hair had been bleached to a "platinum" blonde, but she'd been ordered to the make-up department to be

With Chester Morris,
our leading man
in *Red Headed
Woman*.

Joan Crawford and I
were not only pals,
but she often
demanded that I write
her scripts. One of
them was *Susan
and God*.

Jean's favorite director, Jack Conway, with her favorite husband, Hal Rosson.

fitted with a red wig. She looked about sixteen, and her baby face seemed utterly incongruous against that flaming wig.

Jean didn't seem at all nervous in the presence of the man who was about to skyrocket her into fame; she had that sort of gently sardonic attitude that comes from having gone through the many ups and downs of any budding career in the studios.

Irving, being self-removed from life, dearly loved gossip and he began by asking Jean "How did you make out with Howard Hughes?" "Well, one day when he was eating a cookie he offered me a bite." When we laughed, Jean interrupted. "Don't underestimate that," she said. "The poor guy's so frightened

of germs, it could darn near have been a proposal!"

"Do you think you can make an audience laugh?" asked Irving.

"*With* me or *at* me?"

"*At* you!"

"Why not? People have been laughing at me all my life."

As Jean breezed out of the office, she stopped at the door to give us a quick, bright little nod; a gesture I wrote into the script and still look for every time I see that old movie.

On Jean's departure, Irving said to me, "I don't think we need worry about Miss Harlow's sense of humor."

Next came the choosing of a director, and let me here report that few of them at

118

M.G.M. were very good. With Irving in charge, there was no necessity for a director to have much talent. To direct *Red Headed Woman*, Irving picked on a favorite crony, Jack Conway. He told Jack to read my script and meet with us the following day.

When Jack showed up next morning, he tossed our script onto Irving's desk and said, "I'll direct this if you insist, but take my word, Irving, people are going to laugh at it." When Irving asked Jack in amazement what he *thought* our intention was, Jack was confused. "Look folks," said he, "if you're *trying* to be funny, I'm here to report that a girl like that almost broke up my home once, and believe me it was no joke!"

Irving explained that our heroine was not bent on wrecking the career of any Albert Einstein. "Her victim is as big a dunce as . . ."

"As *me?*" Jack ventured with a squirm.

"You hit the nail right on the head!" said Irving. Jack grinned and accepted the assignment. "But just to be safe," said Irving, "I'll have Nita stay on the set to keep reminding you that the picture's a comedy."

Jean and I had time during that filming to develop a warm friendship. I found that underlying her raffish sense of humor was a resignation unusual for one so young. Nothing would ever surprise Jean. She knew exactly how people were going to react to her; if men were stupid they'd fall for her; if they had good sense, they'd laugh her off. That women were invariably catty toward Jean was largely through a *noblesse oblige* on her part. Jean agreeably supplied them with the shocks they expected.

During the shooting of *Red Headed Woman*, there was one sequence to be filmed on the merry-go-round at the Santa Monica pier. And, as Jack Conway was busy filming another segment of the script, I went out and directed the scene—my first and last attempt at directing.

Every M.G.M. movie was taken out to one of the Los Angeles suburbs for a preview, Irving being the first producer to make use of audiences for constructive criticism. Irving paid small attention to professional critics, putting them down as impersonal theorists; but he read the postcards on which audiences gave their views with the greatest respect; and, guided by them, he would re-edit the movie. In some cases no retakes at all were required, but there were times when those amateur critics demanded as much as a third of the film to be reshot; a procedure which Irving never hesitated to follow.

The initial preview of *Red Headed Woman* took place in Glendale. Irving and I hid out in that suburban audience with our ears nervously tuned for its reaction. And during the first ten minutes we were deeply disturbed, for the audience was as confused as Jack Conway had been. It didn't know whether to laugh at our sex pirate or not; and, as every producer of comedy knows, a half-laugh is worse than none at all. Only after the movie was well along did the audience catch on and begin to enjoy the jokes.

There was no need to wait for postcards on that movie. Irving called me into his office the first thing next morning. "Look," said he, "I'd like you to contrive a prologue that will tip the audience off that the movie's a comedy." I proceeded to concoct a scene that showed Jean describing to her girl friend the all-abiding depth of her love for her married boss; as proof of which Jean revealed a photo of her loved one on a flashy dime-store garter.

Our second preview was in Pasadena and the movie started off with the garter scene. That did it! Laughs began at once and never ceased to mount to the end of the film.

When *Red Headed Woman* was released, it instantly catapulted Jean Harlow into stardom. The picture enjoyed all sorts of fringe successes. It won the award of *Vanity Fair* magazine as the best film of the year; and the London office of M.G.M. reported that the Royal Family kept a copy at Buckingham Palace for entertaining guests after dinner. Among its many distinctions, *Red Headed Woman* made film history because it brought on stringent censorship and caused massive difficulties to the industry for years to come. It outraged ladies' clubs throughout the land, but not because of any episode which might be termed salacious. It was because our heroine, the bad girl of whom all good husbands dream, ended her career as many such scalawags do—rich, happy, and respected, without having paid for a single sin.

Now, one sequence in our movie was a scene in which our redhead was driven home from a shopping tour by a handsome young chauffeur who, laden with packages, respectfully followed his employer upstairs to her bedroom. But after dropping the packages onto a chaise longue, the chauffeur took his redheaded boss into his arms and kissed her in a long, slow fade-out.

The role of that chauffeur, although short, was important, and one morning Irving sent for me to discuss the casting of the part. "We've got a French actor here on a six-month option," said Irving, "but I'm letting him go because nobody can understand the guy's English. His option is up in two weeks, which would be just long enough for him to do the part of that chauffeur. So take a look at his tests and tell me if you think it's worth a rewrite to make the chauffeur a Frenchman."

When I saw the tests in a projection room, I figured the young man's accent wouldn't be too big a problem since his actions were a lot more understandable than words. So he was put into that bit part, in which he finished out his contract and left for Paris, thinking he'd shaken the stardust of Hollywood from his feet forever.

Gable was the man Jean "held" in *Hold Your Man*.

In *Red Headed Woman,* Charles Boyer and Jean shared the beginning of two great careers.

Later, when Irving and I were going through the previews postcards, we found a startling unanimity. Not since the days of Rudolph Valentino had any actor made such an impact on the female audience as had that Frenchman who played the tiny part of Jean's chauffeur. None of us involved in the picture was aware of that young actor's power to enchant. It took those suburban housewives to advise Irving that his French accent was even an asset.

Irving immediately cabled his Paris office to send the actor back to Hollywood. His salary, while under option, had been $250 a week. His new contract called for ten times that figure on a two-year guarantee. And for Charles Boyer that was merely the beginning. There were any number of such thrilling experiences in my eighteen years at M.G.M.

Mr. E and I occupied a house on Elm Drive in the heart of Beverly Hills, an area that resembles any prosperous Midwestern suburb. Its architecture was home-like and its garden well manicured.

Across the street from us was a charming cottage of Cotswold design where Humphrey Bogart lived with his not-so-famous actress wife, Mayo Methot. But life on our block would never be dull. In the early 1940s Lauren Bacall would be on the horizon as a zooming star and the next Mrs. Humphrey Bogart. In fact all Beverly Hills was a mish-mash of marital unrest, frustrated ambition, and

Captains Courageous brought Spencer Tracy, Freddy Bartholomew, and Lionel Barrymore together. Lionel had small interest in children, but he considered Freddy to be civilized.

professional jealousy, all of which I could easily escape because the studio became my home.

All M.G.M. was divided into two parts. Its main section was given over to executive offices, projection rooms, enormous sound stages, wardrobe and make-up departments, dressing rooms, and the mysterious laboratories for the processing of film.

A broad avenue ran through the main lot. It was known as the "Alley," and through it flowed the lifeblood of the studio. There was a constant parade of actors on their way to sound stages; Irving en route to projection rooms accompanied by a group of aides; other producers, followed by galleries of "yes men," of which Irving had none.

My office was in an old cottage; a relic of the time when Culver City was a low-income residential district. I shared it with Lionel Barrymore, who suffered from arthritis and couldn't negotiate a long flight of stairs leading to the dressing rooms. Next door was a cottage that housed the school for contract kids. Mickey Rooney and Judy Garland used to dash in there and out at odd hours making a lot of noise, causing Lionel to gripe with monumental indignation.

Lionel was gifted in many different ways; he composed a symphony that was played by the Minneapolis Symphony Orchestra; he turned out some very professional dry-point etchings. And Lionel was the only actor I ever knew who, when he forgot his lines, would

Two collaborators, Ben Hecht and Charlie MacArthur, with Helen Hayes and her mom, "Brownie," the greatest of all stage mothers ever!

They said that Garbo could never play farce. But Greta fooled them when, with Lubitsch directing and Melvyn Douglas as her co-star, she played *Ninotchka*.

Tallulah was too mercurial ever to settle into Hollywood. After filming *Faithless* with Bob Montgomery, Tallu took off like a skyrocket. I could seldom keep up with her, but I said goodbye to Tallu from the pulpit of St. Bartholomew's on Park Avenue, since I had been chosen best equipped to speak a cheery funeral oration.

extemporize others that were totally in character. It used to amuse me to hear some second-rate scrivener fume about Lionel changing his script, because Lionel generally improved on it.

When the writers were all moved into the Thalberg Building, a directory in the downstairs lobby listed, at one time or another, every important American, English, French, and Hungarian author in the world; Zoë Akins, Maxwell Anderson, Michael Arlen, Vicki Baum, Robert Benchley, Stephen Vincent Benét, Scott Fitzgerald, Robert Flaherty, Moss Hart, Ben Hecht, Samuel Hoffenstein, Sidney Howard, Aldous Huxley, Christopher Isherwood, George S. Kaufman, George Kelly, Frederick Lonsdale, Charles MacArthur, Ferenc Molnár, Dorothy Parker, S.J. Perelman, Ernö Vajda, and John Van Druten.

Those authors were signed on short-term contracts that in most cases were never renewed; for there is a knack about dramatic writing, which some very legitimate talents can't master. The studio's product was actually supplied by only about ten percent of its writing staff. The most reliable were women: Frances Marion, Bess Meredyth, Sonya Levien, Vicki Baum, and Jane Murfin. The three latter had sound literary backgrounds; on the other hand, Frances Marion originated some of the best of the M.G.M. films by talking her plots out in conference, after which the scripts were written by other authors.

Scott Fitzgerald and his adored child, Scottie, to whom he used to write advice he never kept himself.

Irving didn't have a great deal of respect for us scribblers. We irritated him as a sort of necessary evil. "Damn it," he told me one day, "I can keep tabs on everybody else in the studio and see whether or not they're doing their jobs. But I can never tell what's going on in those so-called brains of yours."

While I'd met some of those literary big shots elsewhere, there were many I had had to neglect through sheer surfeit of riches. It was pleasant running into them in the Alley but there was never time enough to make new friends. What leisure I *did* have was spent with Zoë Akins, Charlie MacArthur, Ben Hecht, and Aldous Huxley, with all of whom I'd been on fond terms in New York.

I tried to avoid Scott Fitzgerald, although I'd known him and Zelda intimately in New York, Paris, and on the Riviera. When drunk, their behavior could be downright hazardous or, at best, pretty tiresome. Zelda had a habit of stripping in public, which might be described today as "chutzpah," of which the rule is, "If you've got it, flaunt it." But to flaunt something you haven't got can be a mistake. Zelda's face could have landed her in the front line of the *Ziegfeld Follies*, but she should have kept her bosom strictly under wraps.

Zelda's striptease could be compared with Tallulah's, whose figure suffered the identical drawback. But Tallulah flaunted her nudity through a desire to shock, whereas Zelda felt that hers was delectable.

127

My most horrendous experience with the Fitzgeralds took place one night in Great Neck, Long Island. Scott had picked me up in New York to take me to his country house for dinner. I didn't notice he'd been drinking, but we'd only gone a little way when I realized my error. By a miracle, we arrived at their house without an accident, and, once there, I found to my relief that Zelda was cold sober.

Scott soon disappeared, and then a butler shuffled in and announced dinner. Zelda and I took our places at the table. Presently Scott entered, silent and glowering, and proceeded to turn the latch on the dining-room door. Then, facing Zelda and me he announced: "Now I'm going to kill you two!"

We hadn't time to get up from the table before Scott started pitching things at us from very close range: heavy things; two enormous candelabras with lighted candles, a water carafe, a metal wine cooler and a silver platter with a leg of lamb that the lackadaisical butler had left on the table. Any of those items, properly aimed, actually could have killed one of us. Zelda and I took cover under the heavy oak table.

Then that tall, spindly black butler behaved with more courage than any proper servant might have done. He broke a glass pane in the door, reached through, opened the latch, entered, and grappled with Scott. He managed to hold onto him until Zelda and I could scramble out into the night. We ran across the road to the Ring Lardner house and alerted Ring. He got us safely inside and then went to look for Scott.

It took Ring nearly an hour to find him. When he did, Scott was kneeling on an unpaved road scooping up dust and cramming it into his mouth. "What are you doing?" asked Ring. And Scott, his throat clogged with mud, gasped, "I'm eating dirt to pay for trying to kill those two lovely girls! Those darling girls who never in their lives harmed anyone. And a swine like me tried to kill them!"

It was all very pleasant to be called "lovely" and "darling" and for Scott to admit swinishness, but Zelda and I had put in a very rugged evening.

By 1931 Scott and I were at work in Culver City; Zelda was down south in an asylum for the insane, where she'd been placed for her own safety. (It was there she ultimately met a horrible death in the fire that destroyed the place.)

Poor Scott had quit drinking and, from being a nuisance when tight, had taken on that apologetic humility that is characteristic of reformed drunks. I would hear a tap on my door in the Thalberg Building and know it was Scott because nobody else ever bothered to knock. Scott would enter a couple of steps, then stop. "You don't really want to see me!" he'd say with an embarrassing meekness. I was sorry for Scott because he seemed so alone. He never mentioned a girl friend who popped up after his death.

After a spell of uninspired conversation,

Scott would conclude, "I know you want to get rid of me so I'll go now." Between being dangerous when drunk and eating humble pie when sober, I preferred Scott dangerous. An alcoholic is much more bearable when he's like my dear friend Brendan Behan, roistering his way through to a tragic end, than for his life to fade out, as Scott's did, in one long, dull apologia.

One afternoon a few months before Scott died, he came to our house and wrote a last apology in an autograph book that's arranged according to birthdates. Scott's was September 24, and he composed the following:

SEPTEMBER 24

John Marshall, jurist	1755
Mark Hanna, statesman	1837
Lawson Robertson, Olympic coach	

Libra
The Balance

"Black Friday" financial panic in New York   1869

Charles Brackett

This book tells that Anita Loos
Is a friend of Caesar, friend of Zeus
Of Samuel Goldwyn and Mother Goose
Of Balanchine of the Ballet Russe
Of Tillie the Viennese papoose (Tillie Losch)
Of Charlie MacArthur on the loose
Of Shanks, chiropodist—what's the use?
Of actors who have escaped the noose
Lots of Hollywood beach refuse
Comics covered with Charlotte Russe
Wretched victims of self-abuse

Big producers all obtuse
This is my birthday, but what the deuce
Is that sad fact to Anita Loos

F. Scott Fitzgerald

The set to which I belonged frequented a small café outside the studio, disdaining the commissary, where food was excellent, for bad coffee and stale sandwiches that were spiced with insubordination. Whenever possible, Clark Gable and Spencer Tracy joined us, as did Ted Healy, a comedian who was funnier and rowdier off screen than on. Our group rather lacked girls; the only ones who were welcome were Carole Lombard and Jean Harlow, but, like Clark and Spence, they were generally on the set. As a free agent, I was available. The other writing females never got invited.

We called our hangout the "Trap" and took the same delight in going there that kids do in playing hooky. L.B. tried, without success, to close the Trap, which he looked on as a hideout where we could neglect our jobs. But in many instances it was a case of our jobs neglecting *us*. We'd have preferred to be at work with Irving but he couldn't spend much time on any single project, so while waiting to be called, we indulged in the fairly innocent pastimes of the Trap.

Ted Healy used to work a ploy on girls who showed up at the studio for extra jobs. Using a really superb acting talent, Ted would introduce himself as a professor attached to the personnel department; a scientist who worked along the lines of palmistry except that, instead of merely reading palms, the Professor read the

Scott Fitzgerald had a silly ambition to write movies, at which he failed. I still treasure a poem he wrote me not long before he died.

The one and only Clark. His nickname among us girls at the studio was "The King," while the men dubbed him "The Stud," more out of envy than malice.

The one and only Spence.

A luncheon at the M.G.M. commissary for the Eddie Duchins. We were very gay, for they were on their honeymoon. Little did we know . . .

Judy as Mrs. Vincente Minnelli, gave her director-husband many a headache by not showing up for work. Hoppy and I didn't mind; there was always diversion at hand.

entire body. "You see, little lady," Professor Healy explained, "a body reading is required for all job applicants." Incredible as it seems, any number of those aspirants were gullible enough to place themselves in the Professor's hands. Ted never took advantage of a body reading as many a bona fide analyst is known to do. And when the Professor discovered an interesting case, he might call in consulting scientists; Professors Mahin, Rogers, or Hopkins (Professors Gable and Tracy had to be ruled out as recognizable). But finally news of Professor Healy's clinic filtered into L.B.'s office, and he would have been fired except that, like many movie culprits, he was saved by being in the middle of a picture.

Judy Garland, already a star at the age of twelve, was a compulsive weeper. There are some characters who simply cannot endure success. Judy was one of them. She loved to pace the Alley, stopping all and sundry to whimper over some imagined affront. "Nobody loves me!" Judy would lament. She was "persecuted" by L.B.; her family "neglected" her; even the servants overlooked Judy. "When I come home from work exhausted and ask for a cup of tea, the maid forgets all about it and I have to make it myself." Judy was such a good actress that listeners were frequently impressed. But the more sardonic among us called Judy's tears "a Hollywood bath."

Judy's mental attitude may have been

pathetic, but it turned her into a great bore. And if my memories of her are few, it comes from lack of interest in a character who allowed her destiny to be ruled by petulance.

Judy's disregard for her obligations as a star was appalling. I recall a day at the studio when mild little Vincente Minnelli (Judy's husband of the moment and the father of Liza) was waiting to direct Judy in a scene for *The Pirate*. She was late for work, as usual, and everybody, including a hundred or more extras, had been marking time since nine that morning. Finally, at noon, Vincente was summoned to the phone to learn that Judy required him to get home at once and escort her to an ice-cream parlor for a soda.

By far the most colorful type at M.G.M. was a character named Robert Hopkins. He was listed on the payroll as a writer, but it's doubtful that Hoppy ever put pen to paper. Irving had hired him as a roving gagman, to wander from set to set, ad-libbing jokes wherever a scene might tend to bog down. (Some of Hoppy's remarks went into general usage; his term for the excessively practical Jeanette MacDonald was "The Iron Butterfly.") Hoppy served as Court Jester to Irving and was the pet of the entire studio.

Between Hoppy and me there was an extra special *entente*. We shared the exquisite chauvinism of having been fellow San Franciscans. And now that we were in the coils of Hollywood, our love for Frisco was stronger than ever.

Hoppy had once sketched portraits on the streets of San Francisco using a red-hot stylus on the skins of sheep. One day he found a sheepskin in the property room at M.G.M. and proceeded to give me a demonstration.

With Hoppy, I wrote a movie, *San Francisco*, for Gable, Jeanette MacDonald, and the irrepressible comedian, Ted Healey.

Hoppy and I had been children there at a period when Wilson Mizner had held forth. I had been unaware of his existence, but Hoppy had been more fortunate; he had been a messenger boy on the Barbary Coast where Wilson had run a gambling casino. Hoppy had never ceased to look on Wilson Mizner as an idol. So, in memory of him and the city we loved, Hoppy and I wrote a movie called *San Francisco*. As an added feature we included the Great Earthquake, which, with true Frisco loyalty, Hoppy and I termed a "fire."

Its plot was unadulterated soap opera, told in an underworld setting, and it became one of M.G.M.'s most durable hits. It is still broadcast on the late, late television shows. On March 12, 1972, it was listed in the schedule of *The New York Times*:

1:30 "San Francisco" (1936)
    Clark Gable, Jeanette MacDonald, Spencer Tracy. The works: love, opera and that super-duper earthquake. Grand show.

Its hero was played by Clark Gable; Jeanette MacDonald was cast as the heroine, and Ted Healy provided comedy relief.

One day, Hoppy came up with an idea for a movie for Jean Harlow. Jean would play the daughter of a horsetrader, a girl who had grown up around racetracks. All but the final scene of *Saratoga* had been completed when Jean suddenly came down with a mild ailment, but one that kept her at home, while Jack Conway and the crew "shot around her."

It didn't occur to anyone that her illness might be serious. However, a few of us did wonder what might be wrong, and we decided to give her a call. When the switchboard operator reached Jean's house, she talked for a moment, then hung up and announced to us, "They've taken Jean to Cedars of Lebanon!"

At the suggestion of Clark Gable, the operator called the hospital and got the word that Jean was dead.

Although it is commonly believed that the cause of Jean's death was uremic poisoning, brought on by the excessive use of bleach, in truth the cause was never determined. But the comments of doctors and nurses who had attended Jean at the last seemed to confirm my own suspicions. They all agreed that Jean had refused to put up a fight.

Unlike Marilyn Monroe, Jean was no narcissist. Her sex-appeal was so talked about that it had bored her. When trying on a new dress, she never even bothered to look in a mirror: she knew she would always look the same—terrific.

But her sex-appeal had not made her personal life either happy or successful. She had been married three times, once to a Kansas City playboy, once to a German psycho, and once to a mild-mannered cameraman. All three marriages had been disastrous. She realized as well as anyone that her looks were nothing more than a booby trap for male stupidity, and that it was impossible for her to attract the kind of intelligent and witty man who could be her equal.

Jean had all the sensitivity necessary to a star, but she lacked one of the qualifications for surviving stardom. Jean didn't have enough ego, and so she died of sex starvation.

With one of her husbands, Paul Bern, Jean had been faced with the most horrifying experience any Hollywood star had ever had to go through. Even though their marriage had been one of convenience, Paul Bern adored Jean. Unfortunately there was little he could do to prove it, because he was impotent. When he had married her, he may have felt that—with an inspiration like Jean—he could conquer his problem. But he couldn't; and, as time went by, he tried to assuage his guilt by practices that Jean was too normal to accept. However, she did try to restore his ego by declaring that sex meant little to her. "Just find some other girl who'll be more tolerant," Jean told him. "I won't object; I'll understand."

Probably as a bluff, Bern agreed. To bolster his pretenses, he told Jean one evening of a rendezvous he'd made. As he left for his date, she kissed him tolerantly and wished him good night.

The next morning, Jean found a note that had been slipped under her door, reading:

Dearest Dear—Unfortunately this is the only way to make good the frightful wrong

I have done you and to wipe out my abject humiliation—I love you.

Paul

You understand that last night was only a comedy.

Puzzled, Jean went to Paul's bedroom to ask for an explanation. Bern lay sprawled on the floor in a pool of blood, with a bullet-hole in his head. In the very apotheosis of masochism, he had killed himself standing nude in front of a full-length mirror.

There were other "great legends" of Hollywood that were not all so glamorous as Hollywood's publicity tried to make them. Weekends at the glorious Hearst estate called San Simeon were fraught with suspense. As a result of William Randolph Hearst's Spartan regimen, the smuggling of liquor became an exciting pastime for his guests, most of whom delighted in dramatizing W. R. as a spine-tingling bugaboo.

On arrival, a guest would be met by a servant, who would unpack the luggage and confiscate any bottles, which would be returned only on one's departure. Fortunately for many imbibers, the loyalty of many of W.R.'s servants was not undying, and a well-placed bribe could take care of the problem.

But there were other hazards at San Simeon that I considered more serious than getting caught red-handed with a tot of gin. W.R. kept a collection of wild animals in rather insecure

500
LBS.

Weekends often found us at the Hearst estate of
San Simeon. (Left to right, William Randolph Hearst,
Marion Davies, with unidentified man hidden by
Marion's hat, Mr. and Mrs. Robert Montgomery, and
Chester Morris.)

cages—including a very hungry-looking black panther. Marion Davies' nephew Charlie once remarked, "If you're offered the choice of a second-class hotel, you'd do well to skip San Simeon!"

The bathrooms were frosty, and the fireplaces in the bedrooms were more decorative than functional. Anyone foolish enough to try to light a fire would be met with great clouds of smoke.

In the mornings, I would huddle in the plush canopied bed trying to summon the courage to get up and cross shivering to the bathroom. I knew that I could get plenty of hot water, but I also realized hot water was small comfort in a marble tub, for marble can't be heated.

Meals were ritualized and rather boring. Inevitably I was seated next to W.R., who spoke very little, which forced me to make conversation by praising Marion's movies. Which is probably why I kept getting seated next to W.R.

But there were redeeming factors. W.R. was one of the few truly rich people I've ever known who were infinitely generous and thoughtful. All of a guest's expenses were paid fully by the host. And when on a jaunt, Marion would advise us girls, in her far from disagreeable stutter, to go shopping, and, "If you s-s-see anything you l-l-like, just ch-ch-charge it to your r-r-room. When the b-b-bills are p-p-paid, nobody l-l-looks at them."

Alas, that sort of generosity couldn't go on forever. When it appeared that W.R.'s extravagance was about to lose him his

entire empire, Marion pledged everything she owned to rescue him. It was the true measure of Marion Davies that the possible loss of her jewels and her real estate was no sacrifice at all; Marion's one real luxury was laughter, which was built-in and for free.

I was with Marion at the Santa Monica Beach House when the Hearst lawyers

Frances Marion and I turned out *Blondie of the Follies* for Marion Davies. When Marion smiled, she revealed a truly classic type of beauty.

came to effect rescue. While the meeting was going on, Marion suggested, "Let's l-l-listen at the keyhole and hear what's g-g-going to happen to 'Droopy Drawers'." We listened playfully we listened as the grave legal counsel presented their complicated plan. Fortunately, it worked.

Marion had a pet joke for each of her friends. Mine was that I was her illegitimate child by Calvin Coolidge.

The host and hostess of San Simeon were as warm as the place was cold. There are very few great lovers in the annals of history, but William Randolph Hearst and Marion Davies have to be among them. They could only be parted by death.

It was on New Year's Eve of 1950 that

Wilson and A.L. If this seems almost too idyllic . . . it was!

Adele Astaire, then Lady Cavendish, Lord Cavendish and Hoppy enjoyed many a social occasion at Santa Monica Beach.

Marion led a small group of her friends to their home in Beverly Hills. Before entering, Marion warned us, "Droopy Drawers can't t-t-talk, so don't ask h-h-how he is. Just m-m-make conversation as usual—you know, b-b-be idiotic."

By the Next New Year's Eve, Marion was alone, and she never even got to tell "Droopy Drawers" goodbye. His body was spirited away by the Hearst family while Marion was under sedation.

My sixteen idyllic years of working for Irving Thalberg were brought to an end with the production of *San Francisco*. Just before Hoppy and I finished the final script of that movie, Irving died. His death while still in his thirties had been on its way for a long time. For years doctors had warned

140

Irving to slow down, but his attitude had been: "I'd rather die of overwork than be bored to death by inactivity."

Irving had been stricken soon after he had returned from a heart cure at the German spa of Baden-Baden. It was not heart failure, per se, that brought about his death; Irving died of pneumonia as happens in many such cases. The news plunged all Hollywood into deep despair, and it caused Hoppy to sentimentalize proudly, "It wasn't the little guy's *heart* that failed him!"

With Irving gone, *San Francisco* became the most important issue in the lives of both Hoppy and me. Wilson Mizner had died in 1933, and our movie would be the means of waving both him and Irving a last goodbye.

The day after Irving's funeral, Hoppy and I were disconsolately pacing the Alley. "Irving took M.G.M. to the top of a toboggan. From now on there's only one direction it can go," I lamented.

"Baby, you just said a mouthful!" Hoppy declared, thus repeating a phrase that he himself had added to the English language.

Indeed, it did seem to be a time of many sadnesses. During those days, Marjorie and Eddie Duchin, on their honeymoon, came to the studio for lunch with John Emerson, me, and Hoppy. And this was the last time the five fond companions would ever be together.

Several months later, the Duchins were in New York preparing to welcome a baby. But Eddie had to go on tour, so I planned to join Marge and stay with her until the baby arrived. M.G.M. granted me a two-week leave of absence, and I arranged to arrive in New York at exactly the right time.

I found Marge in great form, buoyed up for the forthcoming ordeal by our mutual friend, Marie Harriman, whose husband Averell was in Washington, holding a high post in the Roosevelt Administration.

Dominating the situation was Marge's mother, "Big Marge." She had been a reigning belle during the Gay Nineties, and nothing could convince her that those snooty days had come to an end. So her greatest concern was that Little Marge should have the most fashionable obstetrician in New York and that the baby would be born in a stylish hospital.

That hospital was located above the Colony Restaurant, a favorite hangout for the élite. The majority of its clientele were either alcoholics bent on sobering up, hypochondriacs pampering their egos, gourmands trying to reduce, or middle-aged beauties hiding out for a facelift.

Then, just before time for Marge to enter the hospital, I was called back to M.G.M. on some emergency. I was bitterly disappointed not to be with Marge when the baby came, and we said a rather melancholy goodbye at the station.

"It doesn't make very good sense to go into that rowdy hospital to have a baby!"

Marge was described by *Vogue* magazine as a "Beige Beauty."

Eddie Duchin, an idol to music lovers and to Marge.

Marge said uneasily. Sharing her apprehension, I agreed, boarded the train, and we waved each other goodbye through the window. It was the last time I ever saw Marge.

About a week after I reached home, Marie Harriman called up with good news; the baby was a boy, and Marge was so well that the obstetrician had been able to leave for a hunting trip in the wilds of Canada.

But ominous news came over the phone two days later. Everything was *not* so fine with Marge. Complications had developed that indicated neglect by the doctor, who couldn't be reached. And the next day, Marie called to say that Marge was dead.

Other disasters followed. The obstetrician, his smart clientele frightened away, never returned to practice; almost immediately, the chichi hospital went out of business. Then we learned that Marge's baby had been born with a respiratory affliction.

Little Peter was placed in an iron lung, but it still remained doubtful that he could survive. Eddie, inducted into the army, was called away on duty. Big Marge, plunging into a state of permanent hysteria, was capable of grabbing the baby out of its iron lung to coddle him; she might actually have coddled him to death. Marie Harriman was forced to be in Washington with Averell, but she provided little Peter with a nurse, Miss Chisholm, who turned out

Eddie Duchin and his son Peter.

to be the next best thing to a mother.

Peter survived the summer; but, with the approach of winter, New York would be no place for the baby, even in an iron lung. So one day, Marie phoned from Washington to ask if I'd take little Peter in and give him a chance of survival in the California climate.

Transporting that iron lung to California was a problem; it had to be brought out by train, in a compartment provided with helium gas. It was war time, when helium gas was requisitioned by the Army. However, in that matter of life and death, Ave was able to get a special permit for the supply.

The baby's trip was one of the most difficult feats of transportation of the entire war years. For there was a danger that the helium might be cut off when the car entered a tunnel. But Ave owned a railroad, so he was able to route a car from New York to Los Angeles without going through a single tunnel. And the trip took eleven days.

I met the train, accompanied by Los Angeles' foremost pediatrician and an ambulance equipped with another iron lung. Peter was whisked into it and gotten safely to a hospital. There a couple of consultants joined the pediatrician; and, after examining the baby, they informed me that Peter couldn't live more than a few weeks. Never having had any experience with babies, sick or well, I believed the specialists. But, from that point on, Nurse Chisholm took over and decided she

Aldous, Peter, Nurse Chissie, and I did what we could to make up the loss of Peter's lovely mother.

wasn't going to let little Peter die.

We were advised that the baby be gotten into the dry desert air as quickly as possible. The nearest point was Palm Springs, and there I rented a bungalow for Peter and Nurse Chissie.

After a few weeks, Chissie risked taking Peter out of the iron lung and found he was able to breathe for a few minutes before starting to gasp. Little by little, those minutes were extended.

Six months later, our pediatricians were

utterly amazed that their patient was still alive. And their respect for Chissie had so mounted that she was allowed to take full charge of the case.

Two years went by, and Peter was finally able to leave the iron lung for good to join his father in New York, where Eddie's band was holding forth in the ballroom at the St. Regis.

I now think back to that dark period when we all felt that, if Peter survived at all, he would be a weakling. But we were wrong. Today, thanks to Nurse Chissie and the desert air of California, that frail little baby has grown up to be a favorite bandleader for the Beautiful People, an all-around athlete, and even a target for the gossip columns that once barred his Daddy from the Social Register.

Not so long ago a headline in a certain scandal-sheet reported "Peter Duchin Bounces Interlopers from Swank Night Club and Quells Riot." To quote from the Epistles of Horace, "*Nil desperandum.*"

Father and son.

6

WOMEN
TO REMEMBER

Helen Hayes

For Helen Hayes, my friend from
girlhood, I wrote a rowdy play called
Happy Birthday.

I started life clutching in my childish fist
a front-row ticket to that great
melodrama, The Twentieth Century. I
met thousands of its fabulous cast,
backstage, but my roster of close friends
excluded exhibitionists. My heart was
touched by characters like Irving
Thalberg who, largely responsible for
Hollywood's golden era had created the
majority of its stars, yet always chose to
remain in obscurity. His career was no
ego trip but an exciting game played for
his own satisfaction.

My close relationship with Helen Hayes,
from the time we were girls, is based on the
fact that I find her much more diverting as
a human being than as the First Lady of
the American Stage.

Helen was pushed into the theater at the
age of seven without *ever* having been
stagestruck. She became a Broadway star
at fifteen but *never* realized she'd done
anything unusual.

Back in 1928, a New York producer,
Edgar Selwyn, was trying to bring *G.P.B.*
to Broadway as a comedy (without music)
and he had run into a snag. After
auditioning dozens of prototypes of the
blonde heroine, Selwyn realized it requires
a very special talent to play a dumb blonde
without making her tedious.

At length a team of young actors named
Mr. and Mrs. Alfred Lunt, approached
Selwyn with a suggestion; a young actress
who had recently attained stardom in a
tragi-comedy called *Coquette*. Selwyn
demurred. "Little Helen Hayes couldn't

even suggest this character. Why she's a virgin!"

So Selwyn passed up an opportunity to make theater history while the role Helen should have played went to an ingenue who was anything but a virgin. There was a bitchy story going around Broadway about that young actress, saying that, when she was about to be married, she had asked Tallulah Bankhead in wide-eyed innocence, "What can I do to prevent getting pregnant after I'm married?" And Tallulah had answered throatily, "Just what you're doing now, old dear!"

At the time Helen was turned down for *G.P.B.*, I didn't know her; but we were bound to meet sooner or later, because I was addicted to the zany young humorist, Charlie MacArthur, who had fallen in love with her.

In those days, Charlie was being courted by the self-appointed wits of the Algonquin Round Table, and because they were persistent and Charlie was easygoing, they sometimes hooked him. But Charlie—knowing that their attitude about his fiancée was "How could a sophisticate like Charlie ever have fallen for that dumb little Hayes girl?"—felt uneasy about taking Helen into their midst. Charlie failed to realize that Helen was much more sophisticated than those Round Table show-offs. She knew they required somebody to listen while they talked big, so she was playing her role to the hilt as a starry-eyed listener.

After Helen married Charlie, I became a regular visitor at "Pretty Penny," their home across the Hudson in Nyack. It was then I came to understand that underneath her sentimental, homespun exterior, Helen had a rollicking Irish sense of humor. How else could she have held onto Charlie, when all the sophistication and wit of Dorothy Parker had failed?

The event that really cemented my friendship with Helen took place one day in 1940. Charlie had taken the two of us to 21, and during lunch Helen began to complain about two noble characters she'd been playing: Queen Victoria and Harriet Beecher Stowe. "I'm fed up with being so grand," said Helen, and then she asked, "Why don't you write me a really rowdy play where I can kick up my heels?"

As a matter of fact, I'd had just such a play in mind for some time. I hadn't connected it with Helen, but now I did. "How would you like to play a drunk?" I asked. Charlie pricked up his ears at once, but Helen looked a trace bewildered. "Did you say a. . . drunk?" she inquired. "A frustrated teetotaler who resents anybody having fun. But one evening she gets gloriously tight and, during a twelve-hour bender, turns into such a sympathetic human being that she straightens out her life and lands the husband of her dreams." Charlie's enthusiasm mounted. "A sort of Cinderella with booze!" he exclaimed. "That would be just fine," said Helen. "Go ahead and write it!"

But before *Happy Birthday* went into

Helen and Charlie on their honeymoon.

rehearsal, Charlie began to have second thoughts about our situation. He warned me that doing a show together might bring about an end to our long friendship.

Charlie was wrong. What I admire most in life is an expert; any expert. Had Richard Nixon only been a *smart* crook, I could even have admired him. Helen and I had both been pros since the age of seven. Her rating as an expert came fully to the surface when Rodgers and Hammerstein, who produced *Happy Birthday*, ordered changes in the script that I felt were wrong. I consulted Helen,

who agreed with me, but she decided the only way to prove we were right was to go ahead and make those changes. They were disastrous and lasted for only one matinee performance. As an expert who knew her job and could understand mine even better than our eminent producers, Helen became pretty special in my eyes. She played *Happy Birthday* on Broadway for eighteen months, an even longer run than her previous record in *Victoria Regina.*

During the closing years of Charlie's life, he was desperately ill, and Helen counted on me to watch over him when

Helen longed to play Lady Mendl,
based on the biography, *To the One I
Love the Best,* by Ludwig Bemelmans.
Bemmy, Charlie, and I tried to write
that play, but we never stopped
talking long enough to get anything
down on paper.

she had to be in the theater. I was their
house guest in Palm Beach while Helen
was acting at the Playhouse there. One
night when I was alone with Charlie, he
suddenly lapsed into a coma, and
panicking, I phoned for a doctor.

When the doctor met his famous patient,
he was tremendously impressed. After
examining Charlie, he beckoned me into
an adjoining room to pose a problem. His
hospital was allied to a Church, and he
didn't want to take Charlie there if his
religious precepts might conflict. "What is
Mr. MacArthur's faith?" the doctor asked. I
was somewhat reluctant to report that
Charlie didn't have any faith at all, so I
suggested that he try to rouse Charlie and
ask him.

The doctor gently shook Charlie and
asked, "Mr. MacArthur, what is your
religious faith?" Charlie raised one weak
eyelid and answered, "I am a phallic
worshipper." At which he slipped back into
a coma, and the square old doctor went
into a state of shock.

During Charlie's last illness, there were
times when he begged Helen that when his
time was up, she would spare him the
barbaric ordeal of a funeral. "If you do that
to me," he threatened, "I'll come back and
haunt you!"

But the day after Charlie died, Helen
called me. "I may be doing something
terrible," she said in deep distress, "but I
just can't overlook all the friends who
want a chance to say goodbye to
Charlie." Helen had consulted Ben

Hecht, who agreed with her about a service for Charlie, and asked if he might read a farewell message.

In deference to his pal, Ben's eulogy was anything but sad. However, in the midst of it, a large floral wreath that hung on a curtain behind Ben started in an uncanny way to sway back and forth. Helen and I looked at each other aghast, thinking it might be that Charlie was letting us know his disapproval.

A particularly strong bond between Helen and me has always been our adoration for New York City. One day in the Fifties, I was preparing to leave for Montecatini, where I had taken a cure every summer for forty years. That year I was more impatient than ever to get away from the summer heat, crime, and labor troubles of Manhattan. So I was a little surprised when Helen asked "Why don't you skip Montecatini and stay home this year?"

I reminded her that I required a cure to prevent arthritis.

"You've no more arthritis than a lizard. You're just looking for an excuse to run away from New York."

Helen had a point; and, always ready to flaunt a worthy cause, she followed it up. "All the things that have made our lives here so fascinating still exist. They're merely buried under a mass of --"

"Garbage," I interrupted, "with the garbage men on strike." Helen was not amused.

"Do you know any garbage men?" she asked. I didn't. "Neither do I," said Helen. "But if they choose to spend their lives coping with garbage, they must be unique. Why not find out?"

Our argument ended in an agreement to spend the summer in New York City and to take up its defense in a book that would shame all New Yorkers for not properly cherishing the most fabulous city in the world.

Helen and I began two years of researching and writing that book, during which we came to share a very fond *entente* with a crew of sanitation men on a tour of picking up garbage. And one time, after saying goodbye to those new cronies, we reached the moody moment that comes at the end of a perfect day. Helen sighed. "I was right about our social life," she affirmed. "I've been spending an awful lot of time with the wrong people."

In doing research for our book, Helen had run across the following accolade to our city written by a Welsh author, James Morris:

"Like so many voyagers before me," he stated, "I was trapped by the Great Port. I loathed it like a lover. The questions it asked I resented; the answers it gave I mistrusted; the spell of it, the chivvying of conscience, the temptations, the delight, I felt to be unfair. Damn you, New York! Damn the bright sweep of your spaces, and the ungainly poetry of your names. A curse on all your archipelago, and on those rough fresh winds off your Bay—which, catching me like an embrace as I stepped

153

Helen and I wrote a paean to our beloved New York, during which we were mightily inspired by a trip on this garbage scow.

(FAR RIGHT)

Arnold Weissberger, our lawyer, about whom the show business of New York revolves, gave a party on my eightieth birthday. Helen Hayes came over from Nyack and, from Mexico City, Dolores Del Rio.

Helen Hayes and Anita Loos present TWICE OVER LIGHTLY New York Then and Now

154

out of the helicopter, so often ravished my spirits, and made my heart sing!''

Helen and I were tremendously affected by the sexiness of that man's tribute. I think it caused us both to be a little bit in love with James Morris. But our affair with him was to have an even sexier conclusion. One day we were alerted by our publisher, who informed us, ''If you two continue to quote that Welshman, you'll have to use a new name. He's had an operation and changed his sex. He is now *Jan* Morris.''

So Helen and I never followed up on our romance.

Today we still look back in nostalgia to the adventures we had in writing *Twice Over Lightly*, to regret the many things we were forced to overlook, the places we never visited, the small museums, the ethnic restaurants, the little libraries, the hundreds of odd specialty shops.

One in particular had enormously piqued our interest. It was an herb shop on Carmine Street in the Village, with the sexy name of ''Aphrodisia.'' We tried to investigate the shop but it was Sunday so it was closed. Helen sighed in reminiscence. ''And now we've missed our chance to learn all about aphrodisiacs!'' she mused.

I told her that I had learned something about them because I'd sent for a catalogue.

''Goody!'' chirped Helen. ''Where is it?''

I fetched the catalogue and read off a list of such erotic nostrums as ''Passion Flower,'' ''Grains of Paradise,'' ''Devil's Shoestring,'' ''Hi-John-the-Conqueror,'' and ''Wahoo Bark.''

Sometime in the future, long after it's too late, Helen and I may visit that shop on Carmine Street and find out what every octogenarian ought to know.

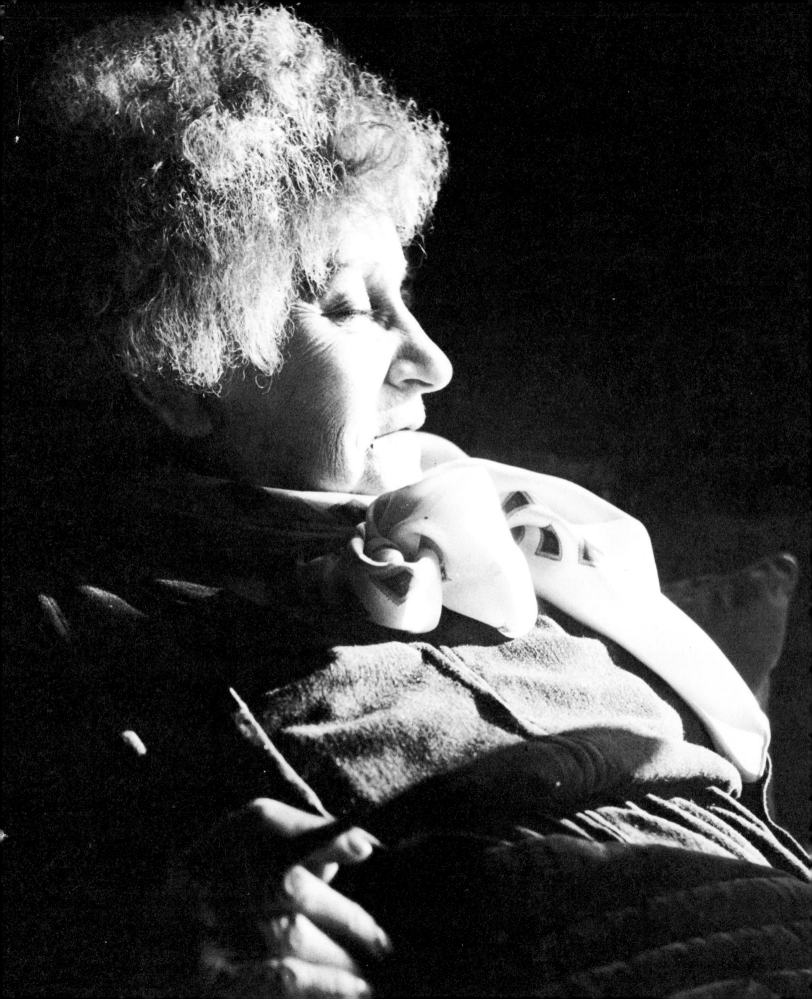

Colette and Audrey Hepburn

Colette was not very well-known to the American reading public when we first met.

But a New York agent was trying to work her novel *Gigi* up as a stage production for Broadway. He was having his difficulties. A dramatization had been made by a French playwright with nineteen stage-settings and a cast of thirty-eight. It was too heavy a load for any box office to carry.

The agent approached me and asked if I would attempt a more practical job. I greatly admired Colette and accepted gladly. I proceeded to work out a version of *Gigi* with a cast of eight characters and only four sets. So far so good. But, from that moment on, the project careened into an obstacle course that periodically threatened it with defeat.

First of all, the stage rights were acquired by Gilbert Miller, who hadn't the least intention of producing *Gigi*. Gilbert's main interest in life was to be an international playboy. At the same time, he didn't want some other producer to acquire a likely property, so he followed his usual custom: paid me an advance of a thousand dollars, tossed my script into the lower drawer of his desk, and went merrily off to Europe.

But luck didn't completely desert the project, for when Gilbert was ready to leave New York, he hired a smart and ambitious young man named Morton Gottlieb to look after his office. In going through Gilbert's desk, Mortie found my manuscript and, as yet unaware of his

Colette, a very great character who brightened my career.

157

Colette's devoted husband, Maurice Goudeket, frequently took us to lunch at Le Grand Véfour, where Colette's favorite table now bears a plaque in her memory.

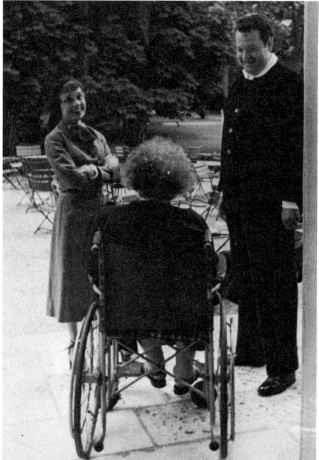

In summertime, Colette left Paris for the Palace Hotel in Versailles, where one day she entertained Orson Welles and me.

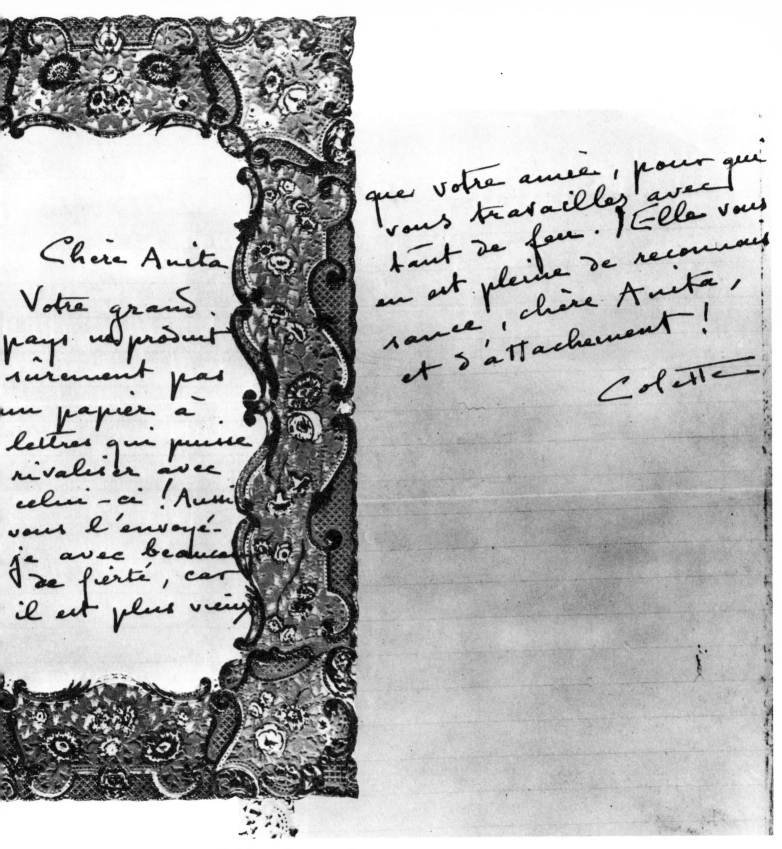

Chère Anita

Votre grand
pays ne produit
sûrement pas
un papier à
lettres qui puisse
rivaliser avec
celui-ci ! Aussi
vous l'envoyé-
je avec beaucoup
de fierté, car
il est plus vieux

que votre amie, pour qui
vous travaillez avec
tant de feu.) Elle vous
en est pleine de reconnais-
sance, chère Anita,
et d'attachement !

Colette

What a treasure! A handwritten letter
from Colette.

159

boss's devious ways, took it on himself to put *Gigi* into production.

Ultimately Gilbert returned from Europe, learned that *Gigi* had been announced in the trade papers, and was so furious that his first impulse was to fire Mortie. But Gilbert's habit of blocking the production of plays was giving him a bad name in the theater. He felt obliged to go ahead with the show, which he did with enormous bad temper.

Early in the procedure, Gilbert was approached by a young composer who suggested writing a score for *Gigi* and co-producing it with Gilbert as a musical. Gilbert hit the ceiling. It was going to be hard enough to find a teenager of outstanding personality who could act such an emotional role. "And now," barked Gilbert, "you suggest she's also got to *sing!*" (At a later period Lerner and Loewe were to prove Gilbert wrong, but he practically ordered Frank Loesser out of his office.)

Gilbert then thought of one more chance to ditch the production. Colette herself might possibly come to his aid by turning down my adaptation. Gilbert sent me to Paris to see Colette.

On arrival there I sent Colette my manuscript and made an appointment to see her after she'd had time to read it.

Our first encounter took place in Colette's apartment in the ancient Palais Royale, where she had long been bed-ridden by a crippling arthritis. I was led into Colette's bedroom by her devoted husband, Maurice Goudeket. Terribly apprehensive about tampering with her classic, I nervously began to talk about the problems of dramatizing it. I presently realized that Colette's mind was wandering, and her gaze was directed toward my feet. But when I slowed down to a halt, Colette spoke up with lively interest. "Where did you buy those adorable shoes?" she asked.

From that moment on we hit it off. Colette was as little obsessed by her career as I was by mine. We talked about everything but the work at hand. It was amazing how much our personal lives had in common. When very young, Colette had been drawn into acting just as I had, not through inclination, but as a means of earning money. As girls we had each had a husband who took both the credit for our work and the money we made. We even shared the same hatred of our long hair and, at the first opportunity, clipped it short.

At the end of our interview, I remembered to ask if we had her permission to use my script for a Broadway production. Only mildly interested she answered, "Of course, of course." For two weeks we met almost daily, but only for gossip. At the end of my visit, Colette wished me Godspeed, and I returned to New York with my bad news for Gilbert Miller.

160

Colette's agreement delighted Mortie as much as it distressed Gilbert, who, losing himself in the pursuits of a Park Avenue playboy, turned the job of producing the play over to Mortie. But the production had hit one snag that even Mortie couldn't surmount. After auditioning all the ingenues on Broadway, he couldn't find a Gigi.

Then one day a cable came to me from Monte Carlo, where Colette and Goudeket regularly spent their summers as guests of Prince Rainier of Monaco. The cable read, "Don't cast your Gigi until you receive my letter."

When Colette's letter arrived, it told of an experience she'd just gone through. She was being taken across the lobby of the Palace Hotel when her wheel chair was blocked by a group of actors filming a movie. The company, on location from London, had brought along a complete English cast. And presently as Colette watched the filming, she noticed a very young girl, far in the background among the extras. Colette instantly recognized that she was Gigi!

Colette summoned one of the film-crew and asked about the girl. "She's here with her mother, the Baroness van Heemstra," said the assistant. "Her mother's over there in the corner." Colette caused the Baroness to be summoned.

The Baroness van Heemstra knew Colette's novel very well, and the idea of her little girl playing that classic role was electrifying. Colette immediately went to the hotel desk and sent me that cable.

By the time Colette's cable arrived, Gilbert was in London. I phoned Colette's message to him and Gilbert promised to look the girl up as soon as the British film troupe returned. Gilbert not only carried through but even showed a first flicker of interest in our project. He phoned me, "You'd better get over here right away!"

I was about to leave for Paris with Paulette Goddard on a holiday, but we changed our plans in order to stop over in London. We were in our suite at the Savoy Hotel when Colette's discovery was announced. The girl came in, dressed in a simple white shirtwaist and skirt, but Paulette and I were bowled over by her unusual type of beauty. After talking for a moment, we arranged an audition for her to read for Gilbert the following day. But after she left, Paulette said to me, "There's got to be something wrong with that girl!" I asked "What?" "Anyone who looks like that would have been discovered before she was ten years old. Something's radically wrong with her."

Well, there was nothing wrong, except the strange fact that perfection is almost impossible for the ordinary eye to see. Beside her appearances as a movie-extra and a chorus job in the long-running musical of *High Button Shoes*, she had been in full view of the London public for two years. She was working at a nightclub where, dressed in a tutu, she displayed the cards that announced various nightclub acts. She had been seen by thousands, but a vision so lovely was blocked out by the average person's sight. It had taken Colette to *see* Audrey Hepburn.

Gilbert listened to Audrey read the role. She didn't do it very well, but Audrey was engaged.

She had been booked to come to New York on a ship, but Audrey had so suffered from malnutrition during the German occupation of Amsterdam in World War II that the poor child didn't even try to resist the first delicious food she could remember. So she gained fifteen pounds on the ship. When Gilbert saw her, he was appalled. He had engaged a sprite who had suddenly turned into a dumpling.

Gilbert, as a gourmand, couldn't believe that his Gigi could ever get down to weight.

Rehearsals began, with Gilbert regarding his ingenue's weight with a skeptical *eye*. But Mortie put Audrey on a diet of steak tartar at Dinty Moore's, next door to our 46th Street Theater. Her pounds slowly began to melt; and to date, they have never returned.

The production, guided by Gilbert's most snobbish expertise, was directed by the eminent French director, Raymond Rouleau. The scenic artist was Lila de Nobilli, whose designs for the Paris Opéra's production of *Carmen* would later become a landmark of art and realism.

But when Lila arrived, the show hit

Audrey was only the first of many international Gigis. A Parisian applicant for the role was turned down as not having any personality. She made good in French movies as Brigitte Bardot.

In 1976, Audrey and I met again at a
luncheon with the Earl McGraths.

another snag. The scenic designer's union didn't allow foreigners to work here. So Mortie put a well-known ploy into effect. He engaged an American stooge, whose name was on the program as set designer, and Lila herself painted the scenery, sneaking into the theater after dark, mounting a stepladder and painting all night.

The rehearsals were mostly carried on in French. Rouleau and Lila spoke no English, and our beautiful Cathleen Nesbitt, who played Gigi's Aunt Alicia, is bilingual. Audrey spoke both English and French, as any girl of European aristocracy would. The stage doorman at the old 46th Street Theater had had a youthful career in ballet, during which he too had learned French.

But the role of Gigi, like that of Juliet, requires the technique of a seasoned actress. In rehearsing Gigi's passionate blowup at the climax of the last act, Audrey remained much more the petulant teenager than a young woman suffering the sharp anguish of a first tragic love affair.

Everybody worked on poor Audrey; Cathleen Nesbitt helped our director; then Gilbert stepped in and hindered. By opening night we were all on tenterhooks. But Audrey's youth, freshness, and tomboy charm simply dazzled the critics.

The following morning, a miracle took place that occurs so very infrequently on Broadway. Audrey Hepburn's name went up in lights on the marquee of the Fulton Theater. And, out of all those birth pangs, a star was born.

(RIGHT) Cathleen Nesbitt played Aunt Alicia, the grand coquette in *Gigi*, and taught her niece the technique of making good with kings.

Cathleen Nesbitt in her youth had been the inspiration for many of Rupert Brooke's poems. She was the toast of London when she played in *Quality Street*.

Gladys Tipton Turner

It has taken a long while for some of the most important things in my life to be recognized. At Santa Monica during August of '33, I scribbled on my engagement pad a notation of an interview with a new upstairs maid. When the applicant showed up, she looked to be in her mid-twenties. She said she had worked for the same employer from the time she was sixteen, which made her seem reliable. That she was pretty was another good point; pretty girls are happy and pleasant to have around. But I was on my way to meet a youth with whom I was seriously planning to spend the remainder of my life, so I very quickly hired Gladys Tipton and went about the business of living.

I've even forgotten the name of that intended mate, but for over forty-three years, my household has revolved around Gladys Tipton Turner. First and foremost, she can be counted on for at least half a dozen laughs per diem, and she has provided spiritual guidance I would never have accepted from a bore.

Soon after joining my household, Gladys discovered there was no Bible on my bedside table. She made me a gift of one and said "I won't work for any lady who don't read a chapter of this every morning." I'd already learned to enjoy her scoldings because they made me feel young, as if I were a child again. So I gave in.

Gladys has one mystic quality, which stems from her religious nature; the

To make my record complete, Cecil Beaton photographed me with Gladys.

167

palms of her hands are marked by stigmata in the form of red spots that intensify when she's in church. She also employs a form of E.S.P., which may have been inherited from a grandmother who was a Cherokee Indian.

One summer in Italy, Gladys dramatically interrupted a conversation to announce, "Somebody's breaking into my house in Teaneck!" About a week later, a letter from one of her neighbors told that thieves had broken into her house and made off with a piggybank full of pennies at the exact moment of Gladys' revelation.

In our forty-three years together, Gladys has constantly invented surprises. During the period when television was in its infancy, I refused to own a T.V. set. Gladys viewed this for what it really was: intellectual snobbery. So that year at Christmas, she spent her entire savings on a television set, which shamed me out of my stupid bias.

We went through some rugged ordeals in California during World War II. Because gasoline was rationed, we could make only one trip a week for shopping. Gladys would drive me to Beverly Hills where it took an entire day to attend to chores. At that time no restaurant in Beverly Hills was available to blacks. "Let's take our lunch along and pretend we're on a picnic," Gladys would suggest tactfully, not wanting to bring up a point of which I, as white, felt terribly ashamed. She is a very great lady.

When Gladys was a child in the cotton fields of Tennessee, she was stricken with a terrific urge to see the world. It could only have been Fate that caused her to share her wanderlust with mine.

168

On quitting Hollywood, I took Gladys to New York, but before checking into the Waldorf, I was called into the office and informed that blacks weren't allowed to live in the hotel. Appalled, I argued that I'd previously visited there with another colored maid. "That was quite all right, Miss Loos," said the manager, "because the other girl was so light she might have passed as a Cuban." Burning up over that injustice, I phoned the Plaza Hotel and was told to come right over.

In short time, Gladys became the pet of the Plaza, even though she constantly badgered them in my behalf. One week she detected an overcharge of ten cents in the hotel bill; but, instead of taking the small matter up with a cashier, Gladys went to the manager. Thinking naturally that I had sent her, he asked, "Is Miss Loos Scotch?" "No," said Gladys, "I am."

In wartime, when butter was rationed, Gladys used our ration tickets to augment a supply. She kept it on a window sill, but one wintery day a gale blew our butter onto the terrace below. Gladys' strategy was to phone down to a bellboy that Miss Loos' diamond bracelet had fallen onto the terrace and to ask him to retrieve it.

As Gladys directed operations from a window, the boy, his teeth chattering, called up "There's nothing down here, Gladys, but a stick of butter." "That's what I want!" said Gladys. "I knew you wouldn't go into that blizzard for anything less than a diamond bracelet."

There was a period at the Plaza, when Lana Turner happened to be a guest there. Also visiting the hotel was a titled Frenchman who was a movie buff. One day, when bent on phoning Lana Turner, he was connected with Gladys by mistake. She explained that she was the wrong Miss Turner, but Gladys has a line of jive that is downright sexy, and he coaxed her to meet him down in the lobby. "One look at my black face," declared Gladys, "and that Frenchman will leave me be!"

Gladys was mistaken. He forgot all about Lana, and his phone-calls bothered Gladys until he had to go back to France.

Gladys had another international flirtation in Paris. Every day when she reported to my suite at the Hotel Lancaster, she brought me a red rose. "A foreign gentleman brings me one every morning," she explained. But she didn't know his name.

One day in the lobby, Gladys nudged me and pointed out her admirer. He was Vittorio de Sica.

Gladys' social activities are so extensive that an antisocial type like me doesn't try to keep track of them. One time we were in Boston with Helen Hayes for the tryout of *Happy Birthday*, and late one night found ourselves in Helen's suite at the Ritz going over script changes with our producers, Oscar Hammerstein and Richard Rodgers, and our director, Josh Logan. Gladys was serving supper.

During general conversation, Oscar brought up the name of Boston's Mayor

Gladys is as social as I am not.
At a costume ball in
Harlem's Les Seize Club, she
and her husband went as
Mrs. Abraham Lincoln and
General Grant.

Curley, who, in the past, had had difficulties with the law. I'm afraid we spoke of His Honor without much respect, for presently Gladys interrupted. "I don't think you should joke about Mayor Curley! He's one of the nicest gentlemen I ever met."

"Where did you meet him?" asked I.

"At his office. We had a lovely talk."

"About what?" Helen inquired.

"Well, he said he never had time for the theater. So I offered to tell him the plot of *Happy Birthday*. And he buzzed his secretary and told her not to let anybody interrupt."

"But how did you even happen to *be* in his office?" asked Dick Rodgers.

"Well Mr. Rodgers, this is the first time I've come to Boston, so naturally I had to pay my respects to the Mayor."

Gladys is one of the few moderns to whom *noblesse oblige* has any meaning at all.

One momentous day in '58, Gladys came to me and said, "Miss Loos, I have a godchild up in Harlem whose home has just been burned out by a flash fire. Do you mind if I take her in until the family finds a place to live?" As we have a large apartment, I agreed.

On the following day, I heard an unfamiliar laugh in the hall and went out to investigate. Preceding Gladys down the corridor was an enchanting little creature who toddled forward and threw her arms around my knees. That situation might have been in any television soap-opera,

except it was for real, and I was hooked.

I kept putting off the time when Gladys' godchild would go back to her family, using one excuse after another. Finally, I faced the situation head-on. I had once met the little girl's grandmother at the Y. W. C. A. in Harlem, where she had been a secretary, so I called her up. "I don't know how to tell you this," I said, "but I simply can't part from your grandchild." Grandma thought a moment and then said, "There are six more children at home, and they're driving their mother up the wall. Possibly the matter can be arranged."

Anyway, the matter was arranged, and the child joined Gladys and me.

Our first problem concerned the little girl's name. She had been christened "Gladys" after *my* Gladys. But one of my close friends is Gladys Shelley, the song writer. To designate the three as Gladys the *First, Second,* and *Third* would be cumbersome. So I hit on the notion of calling our small Gladys by her family name: "Miss Moore."

The three of us are never separated. Miss Moore has made eight trips to Europe. She speaks really good Italian and, because she went to a bilingual school in New York, her French is passable. When Miss Moore was eight, we enrolled her in the New York School of Ballet, which is guided by Balanchine. During three years, she danced in *The Nutcracker, A Midsummer Night's Dream,* and *Harlequinade.*

We go everywhere together. Here we are in Venice with Chris Alexander.

But Miss Moore's accomplishments are secondary to a sense of humor that hits me at times with a violent repercussion.

One morning when Miss Moore was eight, she rebelled against taking her bath. So I asked, "Do you know how a little girl smells when she doesn't take her bath?"

"Yes," admitted Miss Moore, "she smells like Paris."

I have constantly been amazed by the sophistication of Miss Moore and her little companions. One day when she was only ten, Miss Moore returned home with a song she'd just learned on the school bus.

For four seasons, Gladys' namesake danced in Balanchine's New York City Ballet.

It went:
I wish I had a nickel;
I wish I had a dime;
I wish I had a lover boy
To kiss me all the time.
My mother took my nickel;
My father took my dime;
My sister took my lover boy
And left me Frankenstein.

Luckily Miss Moore's moral sense is as acute as her sense of humor. I once took her to see the Easter spectacle at Radio City Music Hall. While the mechanical organ blasted out with "Holy, Holy, Holy," we watched the Rockettes parade down the aisle garbed as nuns, in pancake make-up and false eyelashes, holding aloft fake Easter lillies. Presently Miss Moore leaned over to ask me in a whisper, "Miss Loos, does God *like* this sort of thing?"

The off-beat environment in which Miss Moore lives hasn't affected her sound sense of values. She gives more consideration to the class play in which she has the bit part of a policeman than to a Balanchine ballet. And she sees no difference in status between Helen Hayes, Lillian Gish, and the lady who scrubs the floors of a Friday.

But she has a great contempt for an unfortunate woman who teaches New Math. One day I tried to straighten Miss Moore out on that subject. "Little girls who don't do their homework never get to be famous." Miss Moore, as usual, had an alibi. "That teacher of mine knows all the answers, but she'll never get famous for understanding New Math!"

Miss Moore can outsmart both Gladys and me on every turn. When naughty she uses an argument for which, as yet, we have found no rebuttal. She lays the blame on the Devil. How can we disclaim his machinations when she learned about them in Sunday School?

I've so little resistance to Miss Moore's wiles that she gets away with murder. So of course she treats me contemptuously as her Number One Easy Mark. But Gladys, who makes her pay roundly for the Devil's evil ways, is naturally regarded with adoration.

Through Gladys I attained kinship with two writers I'd never appreciated; Dorothy Parker and Lillian Hellman, who—as they explain in their memoirs—appreciate blacks above all other Americans.

And in addition to all Gladys' other virtues, her cookery is sublime.

Here we are today, with the addition of a fourth member. His name is Jimmy, but he is only on loan from the McGraths.

These Hollywood literati include (left)
the great Louella, in a formal pose, and,
more informally at New York's Stork
Club, Bob Sherwood, the Oscar
winning scenarist, the writing team of
Garson and Ruth Kanin and A.L.
We are celebrating the advent from
Paris of René Clair and his wife, Bronja.

My niece, Mary, took after her Auntie Anita insofar as movie acting didn't tempt her. She preferred to write and, in 1976, her two books *The Beggars Are Coming* and *Belinda* had sold over a million copies.

Lily Pons used to boast that she was taller than I was. A snapshot of us in the alley at M.G.M. proved Lily to be right.

178

To Netsie
all 100%
Marie

Marie Harriman shared with me the problems of Peter Duchin's childhood.

A British matron vacationing in
Palm Beach was so aggressively
romantic that Cecil Beaton inveigled
her into a symbolic pose.

Dellie, playing solitaire at Lismore, her
huge castle in Ireland. Lismore
Castle is spooky. Its hundreds of
windows as counted from the outside
do not tally with the number one can
find within. One gets lost in the count.

Today Dellie is cosier on her windowsill
in Phoenix, Arizona.

181

Lillian Gish, the one great screen siren
who, like Queen Elizabeth the First,
has remained virginal.

Among many others, Lillian and I
share an interest in health. We often
take our cure together in Montecatini.

Gypsy Rose Lee

Gypsy Rose Lee and I had some curious traits in common. Our most sentimental bond was an adoration of Mike Todd, for whom Gypsy had starred in a revue called *Star and Garter*. Mike requisitioned Gypsy's salary, just as he made off with a certain property of mine. But Mike's tactics were so irresistible that Gyp and I both didn't regret a single dime he lost us.

At one time I adapted a French comedy by Barillet and Gredy for Gyp to try out in summer stock. Now, both of us happened to love clothes,

but Gyp was also able to run them up on her sewing machine, which saved money on the production. However, Gypsy couldn't act as well as she could strip, and when she appeared in a dress, the audience kept calling, "Take it off!" So we finally put the dresses and the show away for another day.

But the entente between us went far deeper than collaboration. In early youth we had each appeared in rather basic vaudeville skits, during which period we whiled away some of our childhood hours reading *The Critique of Pure Reason* by Immanuel Kant. *Why?* Possibily as a counter-irritant to the gag lines we were forced to learn.

Paulette Goddard

The sex life of a Hollywood star attains an apotheosis of glamor in the career of Paulette Goddard. She and I often travel together and, glancing at the space in her passport allotted to one's profession, I note that she writes "actress." This is a perjury. Paulette's profession should read "siren," a breed as extinct as the great white auk.

It has always required the brains of a Cyrano de Bergerac to hold Paulette's interest. She has a talent for intelligent raillery that puts men on the defensive. It even posed a hazard to the intellect of H. G. Wells, who paid her court when she was the bride of Charlie Chaplin.

I recall when, only recently, Joan Crawford invited Paulette to join a foursome of which Paulette's date would be chairman of the board of a billion-dollar enclave. Paulette bridled at the invitation. "I've never in my life dated a businessman!" she maintained.

She never has.

Take for example the four brave men who, to date, have faced the perils of marrying Paulette. The first was scion of a wealthy family of the old South who met Paulette when she was a teenage beauty in the *Ziegfeld Follies*. She had been enticed by the young man's love for sport. (Paulette's tennis was of championship caliber even then, as was her skiing on both snow and water.)

But while riding to hounds with her husband's pack, Paulette learned that sport in the deep South was

Paulette in her pre-Chaplin days.

unaccompanied by thought, and that thought, both outdoors and in, was replaced by bourbon. She walked out on Husband Number One and headed for Hollywood on a theory that life there might be less tedious. Already an inveterate scholar, Paulette had learned a lesson by that first experience—the inadequacy of any scion of the rich.

Her second marriage was to Charlie Chaplin, in which Paulette covered the wide distance between a dunce and a God-given genius.

Before he married Paulette, Charlie's social-life had been dismal. His first wife, blonde, vacuous little Mildred Harris, resembled most film stars in being her own best fan. At mealtime she used to set up a rather large mirror behind her plate so she could look at herself while at table. And Mildred's admiration of what she saw there left her speechless.

By that time, important visitors from all over the world had begun to pay Charlie homage. But until the appearance of Paulette, his social gatherings were beset by lethargy.

Charlie's second helpmeet was a somewhat pretty starlet; a piece of Mexicana named Lita Gray. But both those early unions had been the result of unplanned pregnancies; Mildred's was never completed, which simplified a divorce. But to do credit to Lita, she remained Mrs. Chaplin long enough to produce two very fine sons.

But Lita added no glitter to Charlie Chaplin's social life.

It was frustrating to an outstanding dinner guest such as Bertrand Russell to sit next to a dazzling Mrs. Charlie Chaplin, who would announce, for openers, "Lord Russell, don't you think that L. B. Mayer ought to take a trip to Russia and stop communism?"

No such crack would ever come from the third Mrs. Chaplin. Paulette would have realized that L. B. could only have been an argument *for* communism.

It was true that Charlie Chaplin could extemporize a very good show on his own and much of his after dinner entertainment was as funny as the gags he did on film. There was one in which Charlie used to imitate an art critic studying pictures in a gallery. He would commence by examining a miniature that hung about three feet from the floor; Charlie would then proceed along the wall, studying paintings that hung higher and higher until he reached one at the end that required the stature of a giant to appraise. To watch Charlie's reactions as he seemed to grow from three feet to well over six left everyone in stitches.

In Charlie's entourage there was one shining woman-of-the-world, a companion of his days of poverty in London. By now Constance Collier was a famous Shakespearian star.

Paulette, closing the generation gap that separated her from Charlie, latched onto Constance Collier, who was also bored by Charlie's never-ending talk about films.

From the time she was a girl,
cameramen could never resist Paulette.

For Charlie, as the author of his own movie scripts, was given to reading them aloud to guests after dinner. Excellent as those scenarios were, they failed to hold Paulette's attention after several readings. So she used to sit on the floor behind Charlie's big armchair, under which she stashed a bottle of Dom Perignon champagne to keep her alert. Even so, those recitals were frequently interrupted by the snores of Mrs. Chaplin.

However, on marrying Charlie, Paulette became the stepmama of his two little sons, who happened to be equally bored by the importance of their papa. When Paulette moved in, she adopted the boys, not as a mama but as someone much more fun; the French term "copain" is a better description of their relationship than the cold and sexless term of "pal."

Many years after Paulette had moved beyond Charlie's orbit, Charlie Junior dedicated to Paulette the book he wrote about his father; and, after Sidney had become a great sex symbol on Broadway, he still brought his touchier problems as a Casanova to Paulette for her advice.

Paulette's photographs only partly explain her as a siren, for Hollywood produced a great number of beauties from whom men used to run like wolfhounds. Paulette is different.

Constance Collier used to call her "a natural-born honey-pot," to whom adulation was as normal as breathing. So Paulette's reaction was not to dramatize it.

The fact that she gave no

encouragement to suitors prevented Charlie being jealous and so it was that falling in love with the wife of the divine clown took on the proportions of a cult.

One day the most glamorous of international playboys came to me to confess his love for Paulette. "I want to send some flowers to Paulette that will have a special meaning," Count Bosdari declared. "What is her favorite flower?"

When I happened to bring the matter up with Paulette, she said, "Tell him I adore white violets. He'll never find any, so I won't have to bother thanking him."

But Maurice appealed to a San Francisco florist who undertook to force some white violets in a hothouse. It was weeks before his token was delivered to Paulette. After which Maurice waited for a response . . . and waited. I doubt it ever came. Maurice would have done better to have sent white diamonds.

It was during the latter part of that Chaplin marriage that George Gershwin's tragic romance with Paulette transpired. George, at the peak of his fame, had been brought to Hollywood by Sam Goldwyn to compose music for films. And at that time when he was so near to the end of his short life, George fell hopelessly in love. He used

To Anita Loos —

    Being a composer (not a gentleman),
I prefer brunettes. With every good wish,

        George Gershwin

Rhapsody in Blue.   Feb. 18, 1926.

Burgess Meredith starred with Ginger Rogers, but he was once married to Paulette.

to follow Paulette everywhere; came to life in her presence as nobody had ever seen him before.

Paulette inspired one of George's last ballads, "You Can't Take That Away from Me." The lyric by George's brother Ira stated, "The way you wear your hat—the way you sip your tea—the memory of all that—you can't take that away from me."

George, however, was not at all well. He was beset by recurrent headaches of alarming intensity.

One day at a gathering in Beverly Hills, George had a sudden attack of headache that made him scream out in agony. Paralyzed with fright, nobody was capable of action except Paulette, who phoned Charlie in panic and asked what should be done. "I'll get hold of Dr. Reynolds right away," said Charlie.

Now Reynolds was the best brain specialist in the area, and he came at once. He called an ambulance and took George straight into the operating room at the Cedars of Lebanon. Operating on George's brain, Reynolds uncovered a tumor the size of a fist.

Today one might put down his untimely death as one of the countless crimes of that old Viennese menace to humanity, Sigmund Freud. Early in his illness, George had gone to a Hollywood analyst, who came up with the theory that his headaches were caused by his guilty love for the wife of a friend. And George was spending hours on the couch of that Hollywood analyst who was trying to cure a tumor of the brain by a typical brand of Freudian doubletalk.

Early in Charlie's marriage to Paulette, he had been worried by signs of boredom in his bride; to overcome which Charlie set about casting her as the leading lady in his movies. She gave her first big screen performance in *Modern Times* which still brings forth critical acclaim and she went on to a long and successful movie career on her own. But success in the movies never fulfilled Paulette's roving mentality.

Mrs. Chaplin was getting restless, and Charlie learned along with so many others before and after him that any man who looks for tranquility with Paulette will find it in the dictionary under the letter "T."

Paulette's third marriage was to stage and screen star Burgess Meredith. Burgess was young, good-looking, and talented. He had the wit of his Irish heritage and earned a movie star's salary. But Paulette's scheme of life had always been "onward and upward," and for her to supplant the great Chaplin even with a charmer like Burgess was puzzling.

After their divorce, the explanation given by Burgess was that Paulette married him to gain some sort of a tax deduction. Paulette never dignified that cockamamy explanation by a denial. She has always followed the advice of our pal, Lady Mendl, whose credo was "Never complain, never explain." But in a moment of truth, Paulette once told me her bona fide reason for becoming Mrs. Meredith.

"One night, during World War II, I was in New York," she explained, "drinking champagne at the bar in El Morocco, when a man I'd met in Washington stepped up and asked, 'How would you like to go to China and entertain the troups?' " Having left Charlie, she was free, at loose ends; and, being also a little tight, she agreed.

Paulette always accepts an invitation knowing that when she bows out, she can express her regrets with more urgency. But that time she was trapped. The U.S. troops under General Chenault were on the move; and before realizing what she'd done, Paulette found herself in war-torn China, the first and only female among acres of men in khaki. Night after night, the campaign surged about Paulette as she danced on makeshift platforms with the troops.

Now it was only to be expected that those pardners took every possible advantage of dancing with Paulette. And she endured their lack of restraint as best she could. "Those poor boys were on their way through hell," said she, "so how could a girl blame them for being pushy?"

Well, those six weeks of being mauled in China were as if Paulette had spent ten years of hard labor in the dives of Marseilles. Every bead had been rubbed off her ball-gown, and she was left with one urge—to spend the rest of her life as a wallflower.

"I staggered off a plane in California," Paulette told me, "and found Burgess waiting there. The first thing he said was

'Gee, but you look awful!' " His words cancelled out all the creepy double entendre which had nauseated her for weeks. And when Burgess added "Let's get married," it seemed to put a limit on sex for once and all! "I let him lead me straight off to the license bureau!"

Paulette never emerges from an experience, however, without having learned something. And she learned in wartime China that the only troops who treated her with respect and even reverence were black. But when Paulette sentimentalized about that experience in the presence of Miss Moore, the latter remarked "If you ask me, Miss Goddard, I think those black boys were stupid."

Indicating that, in the realm of sex, Paulette has always been old-timey.

To accompany Paulette into her own world as I have done these many years is full of surprises. Women never believe she isn't the hard-working sexpot her jewels and vast worldly goods indicate. The fact is that she completely changes the metabolism of any man she encounters. Unlike the ancient Circe, who turned men into swine, Paulette turns them into pussycats.

During the Spring of 1973, in the first awful week of the Watergate investigation, some journalist wrote, "The only scandalous element lacking in the Watergate affair is *sex*." Well, due to Paulette, it even had that! And now, with Watergate a thing of the past, the incident can be told.

It began in New York one afternoon, when Paulette ventured forth to a Seventh Avenue wholesale showroom to pick up a bargain dress as is her wont. While she was studying the collection, Paulette became aware of a distinguished elderly gentleman who was studying *her*. He presently wangled an introduction through the owner of the firm, in which he happened to be an investor.

Paulette's admirer turned out to be of great wealth, in addition to which he held an important post in the nation's Capitol, ostensibly for his contributions to the fund for reelecting President Nixon. (Otherwise how could someone in a chronic state of intemperance be appointed, as he had been, to our President's National Council for Physical Fitness?)

In order to disguise the gentleman's identity, let us call him "Mr. Miller." But the gay old boy had been given a nickname in his native Western State, where everybody called him "Whoopsie."

To describe Paulette's allure adequately requires only a camera.

194

That day Paulette had scarcely returned to her apartment from the dress-showing when the following telegram arrived:

```
IPMDCKB NYK
2-172587E133 05/13/73

ICS IPMMTZZ CSP

  212PL34500 TDMT NEW YORK NY 74 05-13 1128A EST

PMS THE ELEGANT PAULETTE GODDARD, DLR


NEW YORK NY 10022

PAULETTE, HOPEFULLY YOU'RE MY NEW FRIEND. IT'S KIND OF NICE

TO HAVE A BRAND NEW FRIEND. REALLY AND TRULY WANT YOU ON OUR

ADVISORS COMMITTEE FOR THE PHYSICAL FITNESS AND SPORTS COMMITTEE

FROM THE WHITE HOUSE. KNOWING THAT YOU'RE LEAVING FOR EUROPE

ALL TOO SOON, PLEASE CALL      SOMETIME AT YOUR CONVENIENCE

IN SUITE 501 AND 502 SAINT REGIS HOTEL NEW YORK N.Y.

P.S. PAULETTE HONEY TRY. WANT TO TALK TO YOU. WITH LOVE
```

```
DCD041 903A EDT MAY 12 73 NYL032(0741)(2-073388E132)PD 05/12/73 0741
ICS IPMMTZZ CSP
412PL34500 TDMT PITTSBURGH PA 80 05-12 0741A EST
PMS MISS PAULETTE GODDARD, DLR
NEW YORK NY10022
PAULETTE, I'VE BEEN WAITING AROUND ALL MY LIFE TO BE DISARMED
AND STRUCK BY A BEAUTIFUL GIRL. PAULETTE, YOU'RE DANCING EYES,
YOUR NEAT FIGURE WRAPPED UP IN THAT GREY PLAID SUIT SOME HOW
KIND OF GOT TO ME. PAULETTE I CAN HARDLY WAIT TO APPOINT YOU
AS A SPECIAL ADVISOR TO THE PRESIDENT'S COUNCIL ON PHYSICAL
FITNESS IN SPORTS.    PAULETTE PLEASE CALL
PL34500 SUITE 501 ANYTIME THIS AFTERNOON.            AT
PAULETTE YOU'RE NEAT NIFTY AND NICE AFFECTIONATELY YOURS

SF-1201 (R5-69)
```

Endless phone calls followed with proposals of marriage, which our heroine declined. Men want to marry Paulette on the same impulse that makes a rabbit charge the headlights of a Rolls Royce.

Now during the very time that Whoopsie was hell-bent on supplying a sex angle to the Watergate affair, John Dean, that unfeathered canary, was chirping his tiny heart out in a requiem to our President, a fact that ought to have made Whoopsie cautious of supplying our news media with the headline: *WHOOPSIE MILLER OFFERS POST ON PRESIDENT'S COUNCIL FOR PHYSICAL FITNESS TO—GUESS WHO? PAULETTE GODDARD.*

"Whoopsie shouldn't have sent that telegram," observed Paulette, "until he made sure I'd toss it into a shredding machine." And then she mused, "But it goes to show that a shredding machine is the last item a girl should ever own!"

Raoul Dufy was nearing the end of his life when he was dazzled by Paulette on shipboard.

7

MEN TO REMEMBER

Erich Maria Remarque

Paulette Goddard's fourth marriage made up for all the hazards of the other three. Erich Remarque fulfilled every one of her tough requirements. More than handsome, he was elegant; more than elegant, he was a wit; more than that, his novel *All Quiet on the Western Front* had made Erich very rich. He had become a connoisseur of every amenity—art, women, jewels, food and wine.

Erich's mistresses had included several of the world's most famous professional beauties. In fact, he first met Paulette by chance at a Park Avenue florist's, where he'd gone to order flowers for her predecessor. He sent the flowers, but he asked Paulette to dine, which they did every night thereafter for the fourteen remaining years of his life.

Erich had a gallantry toward women that has now gone out of fashion. But as a European, and German-born at that, he was not quite as bewildered as most men are by the enigmas his bride presented; he merely put them down as "shenanigans," and they amused him. But Erich also considered Paulette seriously as the greatest art object in his collections, more fascinating than his Egyptian bronzes or his Monet water-lilies.

And, in 1971 when Erich finally departed from the special world he created around Paulette, romance must have disappeared from her life forever. In Erich she had met her match and I doubt there's another one around anywhere.

Edwin Hubble and Moe Berg

Before I met him, Moe Berg was a professional baseball player.

During the more than eighty years of my life, I've witnessed a steady erosion in the dignity of Man. I was alerted to the process soon after World War I, when I first went to Vienna. At that time Sigmund Freud was just rising to prominence in the U.S.A., so it came as a surprise that Viennese intellectuals looked on him as a bugaboo. "Why do you Americans listen to that wretched creature?" I was asked. "Don't you realize he's out to dirty the minds of the world? That while Hitler had been brutalizing mankind, Freud was emasculating it? That a Freudian Hamlet, unable to express himself in the sublime terms of Shakespeare, merely hates momma, or harbors a letch for her and either case provides immunity for mankind to follow any sort of snide behavior it can dredge from the lower reaches of its libidos."

The human being of high principle, the Biblical man, the Shakespearian man, has disappeared without leaving any spiritual progeny, although I grant that Ralph Nader may be as spiritual as anyone can be in an ambiance of stale motor fumes and wholesale warehouses. The trouble is that Ralph doesn't exactly elevate the human soul. But in these least inspiring of times, I take comfort by remembering certain great men I've encountered.

I met the astronomer Edwin Hubble at the Observatory of the University of Southern California on Mount Wilson, overlooking Pasadena. Working at M.G.M., I became curious about other stars than the ones at our studio, so I wrote Professor Hubble for permission to visit Mount Wilson. I had expected some sort of a printed pass, instead of which there came a handwritten letter. It started by asking, "Are you *really* Anita Loos?" I was bowled over. That the great scientist was aware of my existence. How smashing!

Ultimately Edwin Hubble and his wife Grace became members of our group, which included Aldous and Maria Huxley, Charlie and Paulette Chaplin. Grace, Maria, and Paulette shared a unique distinction; they were equally as diverting as the geniuses they had married.

In planning that first visit to Mount Wilson, the Huxleys and the Chaplins were included. We all found it ego-shattering to look at the stars through the one-hundred-inch telescope. Manipulating that sensitive instrument to the exact degree to pinpoint a tiny star in the immensity of the universe required great mathematical skill. And it came about that during World War II, the U.S. Army requisitioned Edwin to mastermind bombing schedules for its air attack on Germany.

Edwin uprooted himself from his contact with the universe, from his cozy academic home in Altadena (one of his treasures there was a manuscript by Copernicus in which he had tried to erase the theory that ultimately sent him to prison.)

Edwin took up residence in a shack on the swamps of the Maryland Proving Ground. The dampness raised havoc with his health; Edwin was prone to rheumatism, and he never fully recovered from that ordeal. But his bombing schedules began to win the Battle of Berlin for us. During Edwin's tenure of that shack, a German submarine was sighted cruising the coast of Maryland and an enemy directive was decoded that read: "Get Hubble."

That was when Moe Berg came into Edwin's life, for Moe had been decoding enemy messages for the O.S.S. At any rate, the Germans never "got" Hubble; and, as far as any war can be won, the U.S. won it.

Now I had moved to New York during the war, and when Edwin's work was finished in Maryland, he stopped by there before returning home. He called me up one day to make a date, but it was for something much more important than to say goodbye. "I'm going to treat you to an experience you'll never forget," Edwin told me. And the day he showed up, Edwin brought Moe Berg along.

To the general public, Moe was known

In every sense of the word, Edwin Hubble was fully macho

only as a prominent baseball player. I had never even heard his name. But nobody had to have an interest in baseball to size up young Moe Berg. He was the handsomest male I'd encountered since Clark Gable. But Gable had never stirred my vibrations. I was not interested in the macho world that obsessed Clark—the hunting, fishing, camping, and sleeping in canvas bags. But Moe Berg, over and above his skill as an athlete, was an intellectual, a man of culture whose formative years were divided between the Ivy Halls of Princeton and baseball fields all over the world. He had a special talent for languages, spoke eight of them flawlessly and without accent. Moe could translate languages for his team-mates even in far-off places like Japan.

Edwin admitted to being out-of-line in introducing me to Moe, and particularly in talking about his work as a spy for the O.S.S. I was never to repeat anything that was said or even to mention Moe Berg's name. Edwin only wanted to provide me with a secret account of American patriotism I would never forget.

Urged on by Edwin, Moe Berg told me first hand of his work for the O.S.S. At all times Moe was required to carry a lethal pill in case of capture. He described a certain mission inside enemy lines, where—speaking as a Hungarian professor—he had addressed a conference of atomic scientists in Budapest.

After the war Moe Berg continued his services for the O.S.S., having to live the solitary life of a spy even in peacetime. He could never make contact with other people, had to disappear without leaving addresses or any other clue that he existed. And he continued that same arid life until his death in 1972. In the course of his faceless existence, even Moe's death was nondescript; it was caused by a fall on the staircase of an obscure suburban cottage he inhabited alone.

There has now been a loosening of the restrictions concerning Moe Berg. A biography has appeared. So I can openly boast that I knew him, that I followed his career through Grace Hubble, with whom he ventured to keep in touch whenever his duties took him to Southern California.

Edwin, too, is gone. But in looking back on those two ardent characters whom Professor Freud could never have sullied, I can thumb my nose at that nasty old man.

Aldous Huxley

In the summer of 1926, I was living an extremely hectic existence in New York. *G.P.B.* had been published the previous year and was giving rise to stirring incidents almost every day. I was getting countless letters from people I'd never met; the most exciting of them all was Aldous Huxley. It was datelined Chicago, where he must have been on a lecture tour:

Congress Hotel
14-May-1926
Dear Miss Anita Loos,

I have no excuse for writing to you—no excuse, except that I was enraptured by the book, have just hugely enjoyed the play, and am to be in America so short a time that I have no leisure to do things in the polite and tortuous way. My wife and I are to be in New York for about a fortnight from Monday 17th onwards and it would be a very great pleasure—for us at any rate—if we could arrange a meeting with you during that time. Please forgive my impatience and accept the sincere admiration which is its cause and justification.

Yours very sincerely,
Aldous Huxley

Soon after Aldous and Maria arrived in New York, we met for tea, and I was immediately struck by his physical beauty; Aldous was a giant in height, with the magnificent head of an angel drawn by William Blake. His faulty vision made Aldous appear to be looking at things above and beyond what other people saw. But his chief trait was an intense curiosity; and, while he was the greatest of all talkers, he was equally the greatest of all listeners. Maria, a tiny fragile brunette, was as unusual in her way as Aldous was in his. It was after I came to know her well that I learned the real meaning of the word 'fey'; Maria lived a life of pure fantasy. She studied palmistry, believed in the stars, and

Two great thinkers—Edwin Hubble and Aldous Huxley, as photographed during a stroll by A. Loos.

even in the crystal-gazers of Hollywood Boulevard. At the same time, she protected Aldous from the swarms of bores, pests, and ridiculous disciples who try to attach themselves to a great man, and all the while her unconventional reactions amused Aldous as well as amazed him.

Following that tea party in New York, our correspondence was resumed, and their friendship became a constant factor in my life. After I moved to Santa Monica, the Huxleys came to settle in nearby Los Angeles, bringing their son Matthew, whom I met for the first time. Many complex reasons have been offered as to why Aldous left London—but the explanation is really quite simple. The dry air of Southern California was most soothing to his lungs, which were never robust, and his faulty vision was at its best in the California sunlight, which was still of a pristine clarity. Later on, when smoke and grime polluted the air, the Huxleys' roots were too firmly planted for them to pull free.

They soon collected a group of friends; among the regulars were Edwin Hubble, the distinguished astronomer and theorist of the expanding universe, his wife Grace, Gerald Heard, Christopher Isherwood, Charlie Chaplin, Paulette Goddard, and Greta Garbo.

For years our lives ran along the most pleasant lines. No place in the world provides as much food for laughter as Southern California, with its extraordinary assortment of kooks and goons; its fantastic religious cults—the Four Square Gospel of Amy Semple MacPherson, the Holy Rollers, and the Great I Am were a constant source of amusement to Aldous.

Every Sunday, our group came to my house on the ocean front at Santa Monica for lunch, after which we usually took long walks on the beach. Walking was a favorite entertainment; and Aldous, like the Pied Piper, led us all after him.

Our walking tours set us apart from the majority of Southern Californians, who are so dependent on wheels that they've lost the use of their legs. Any citizen caught by the police using his feet for transportation is suspect. On one occasion, Aldous, out for an evening stroll in Beverly Hills, was stopped by two officers of the law who wanted to know what he was up to. Aldous's reply that he was merely taking the air didn't at

As health freaks, Aldous and Maria Huxley stamped out their own homemade wine.

206

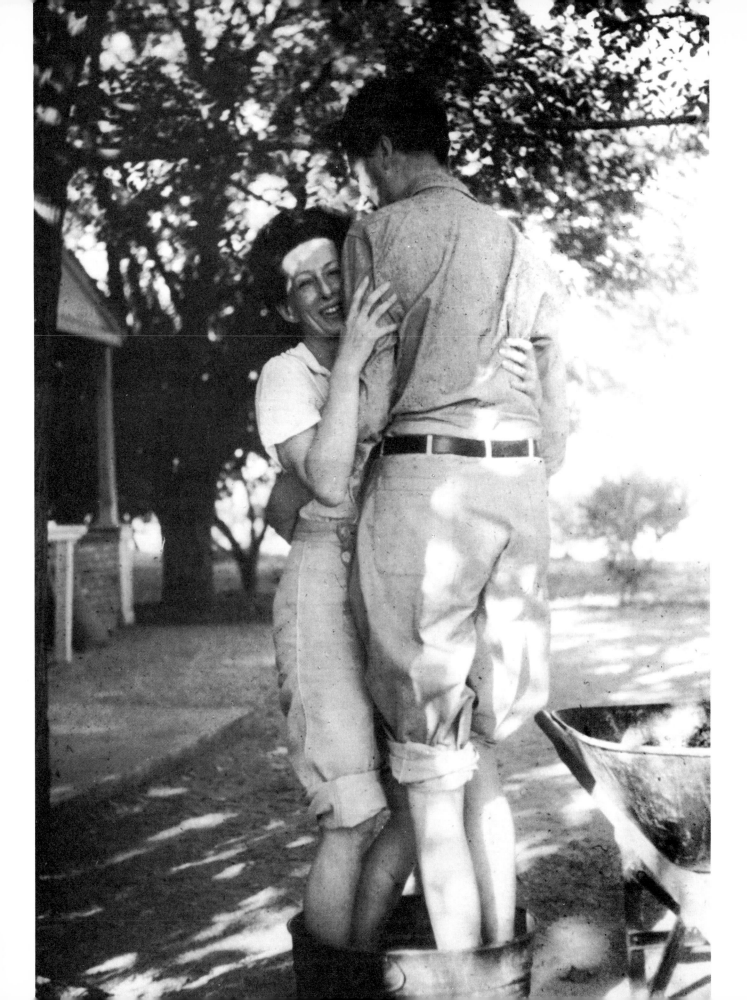

all convince the patrolmen, who ordered him to get off the sidewalk at once or they'd haul him to the station. That near-arrest greatly amused Aldous as a measure of the Southland's *Kultur*.

Aldous and Maria had a childish love for picnics. I recall one particular outing that had a *dramatis personae* so fantastic that it might have come out of *Alice in Wonderland*. There were several theosophists from India, the most prominent being Krishnamurti. The Indian ladies were dressed in saris, which were elegant enough, but the rest of us wore the most casual old sports outfits. Aldous might have been the giant from some circus sideshow; Maria and I could have served as dwarfs; but, with our tacky clothes, the circus would have been pretty second-rate. Nobody would have recognized the glamor of Greta Garbo and Paulette Goddard. To protect themselves from fans who might crop up out of nowhere, Greta was disguised in a pair of men's trousers and a battered hat with a floppy brim that almost covered her face; Paulette wore a native Mexican outfit with colored yarn braided into her hair. Bertrand Russell, visiting Hollywood at the time, Charlie Chaplin, and Christopher Isherwood all looked like naughty pixies out on a spree. Matthew Huxley was the only one of the group who was a mere normally disheveled teenager.

The picnic gear was as unusual as the cast of characters. Krishnamurti and his Indian friends, forbidden to cook or eat from vessels that had been contaminated by animal food, were weighed down with crockery and an assortment of pots and pans. Greta, then strictly a vegetarian, was on a special diet of raw carrots, which hung at her side in bunches. The others could and did eat ordinary picnic fare; but Paulette, to whom no occasion is festive without champagne, carried a wine-cooler.

We had started out in several motor cars, with no definite objective, but it was difficult to find a location where the theosophists could cook without danger of starting a brush fire. We finally found a place that, in the matter of safety, was ideal. The scenery left quite a lot to be desired, for we had chosen the sandy bottom of the Los Angeles River, which—although a raging torrent during the rainy season—was now without water or even dry vegetation. As we trooped down into the hot river bottom, we failed to notice a sign that read "No Trespassing."

Krishnamurti and the Indian delegation set about cooking their rice. And while the remainder of us were unpacking sandwiches, Greta's raw carrots, and Paulette's caviar, we were shocked by a gruff male voice ringing out with, "What the hell's going on here?"

Stunned into silence, we turned around to face a sheriff, or some reasonable facsimile, with a gun in his hand.

"Don't anybody in this gang know how

For Anita
in memory of
her too rare
visits to Llano,
with my best love

AHH

1947

When smog overcame Los Angeles, the Huxleys retreated to the desert.

Aldous' faulty eyesight improved, and he was able to draw a picture for me of the view from his window.

to read?" he demanded.

Aldous meekly allowed that he could read, but still no one got the man's implication until he pointed out the sign. Then Aldous promised that as soon as we'd finished our picnic, we'd clean up and leave the river bottom neat and tidy. It was apparent that his plea was getting nowhere; the sheriff merely glowered and fingered his gun. Then Aldous played his trump card. He indicated the presence of Miss Garbo, Miss Goddard, and Mr. Chaplin. The sheriff's measly little eyes squinted only briefly at the group.

210

"Is that so?" he asked. "Well, I've seen every movie they ever made," said he, "and none of them stars belong in this outfit. So get out of here, you tramps, or I'll arrest the whole slew of you."

We folded our tents like the Arabs, and guiltily stole away. It was not until we resumed our picnic in the garden of the Huxley house that we began to think about the titillating headlines our adventure might have produced:

"Mass arrest in Hollywood! Greta Garbo, Paulette Goddard, Charlie Chaplin, Aldous Huxley, Lord Bertrand Russell, Krishnamurti, and Christopher Isherwood taken into custody."

When the expanding industries of Los Angeles began to darken the air with smog, the Huxleys retreated to Santa Monica, and their home on a hilltop overlooking the Pacific became a source of fun for all of us. The house belonged to an eccentric who had furnished it with conversation-pieces that could have been assembled in no other culture in the world. On entering the hall, one was greeted by an *objet d'art* that had been used to advertise a movie—the larger than lifesized facsimile of King Kong, in whose hairy arms a sparsely dressed cutie was struggling, while Kong looked around for a convenient spot to commit rape. The remainder of the decor did Kong injustice: there was a bar that was an Arabian Night's dream of dowdy grandeur; red lights revolved and blinked down on a large, stuffed crocodile, and there was layer upon layer of tortured motifs cut out of wood with a fret saw. Of course, Aldous could have thrust all those eyesores into the cellar, but he didn't. He felt it would be a shame to dispense with a unique source of amusement in a world filled to the brim with sadness.

During World War II, Aldous's profound sensitivity made him look on its grim course as a matter so personal that it shouldn't be discussed.

I remember the night when Paris fell, and a number of our group came to dine at our house. When Aldous arrived, his face was dead white; he bore the expression of someone who was peering into hell; but the talk was mostly some sort of scientific discussion between Aldous and Edwin Hubble. Nobody mentioned Paris.

Incredible as it may appear, there were times in our relationship when I was able to feel a little superior to Aldous. He once came to me to say that, staunchly as he had remained apart from the movie industry, he now felt tempted to try for a job in it. The Battle of Britain was on in full force; his income was curtailed by it, and his obligations increased. Did I think he might possibly make good in one of the studios? I laughed at his ridiculous humility and told Aldous nothing could be easier than to find him a job. On investigating the new projects coming up at M.G.M., I found one that seemed ideal—a movie version of *Pride and Prejudice*, which was ready for dialogue.

When I informed the producer that the great writer was available, he set up an appointment with Aldous for the very next day.

Very soon after their interview, my phone rang; Aldous was calling, with Maria on the extension, and their mood was that of gloomy resignation.

"I'm sorry," Aldous said, "but I can't take that movie job."

I wanted to know why not.

"Because it pays twenty-five hundred dollars a week," he answered in deep distress. "I simply can't accept all that money to work in a pleasant studio while my family and friends are starving and being bombed in England."

"But Aldous," I asked, "why can't you accept that salary and send it to England?"

There was a long silence at the other end of the line, and then Maria spoke up.

"Anita," she said, "what would we ever do without you?"

"The trouble with Aldous," I told her, "is that once in a while a genius isn't very smart."

To my own particular viewpoint, Aldous' sense of humor outshone all the other facets of his tremendously complex nature. It even came into play at the time when one of those hellish Southern California brush fires had destroyed the home where Aldous lived with Laura, whom he had married the year following Maria's death. He and Laura had barely escaped with their lives, but Aldous' manuscripts, Maria's diaries with their record of the happy, eventful years they had spent together, Aldous' priceless letters from most of the great people of his time, and a library that had been collected during the major part of his life, had all been reduced to ashes. On reading about the catastrophe, I phoned Aldous from New York for a firsthand account. I could sense that he was smiling when he said quizzically, "It was a bad experience, but it did make one feel extraordinarily clean."

I shall always think of Aldous as smiling. One of my most cherished mementos of his is a delicate bottle of Schiaparelli perfume in a fancy pink box made in the shape of a book. On the flyleaf Aldous wrote, "For Anita, one of the few books that doesn't stink."

At first glance, Aldous' companion might seem to be Jackie Coogan. Actually it was only A.L.

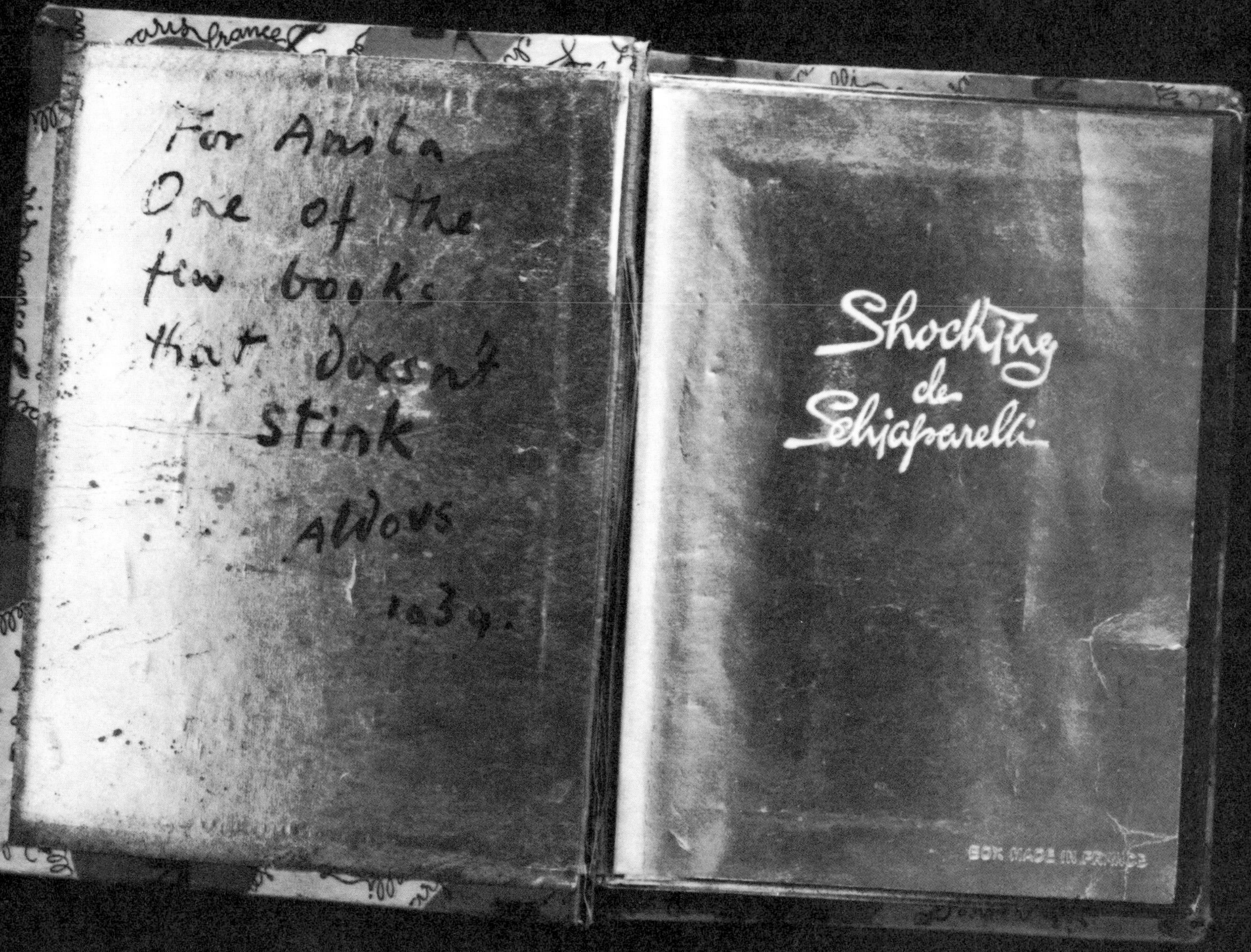

For Anita
One of the
few books
that doesn't
stink
Aldous
1934

Shocking
de
Schiaparelli

BOX MADE IN FRANCE

Ernst Lubitsch

The most sophisticated of all Hollywood musicals were directed by Ernst Lubitsch. But with a genius for dreaming up scenes in which Maurice Chevalier drank slippersful of champagne to either Mae Murray or Jeanette MacDonald, Ernst looked for all the world like a little pushcart peddler.

Concerning Ernst's sophistication, I recall an afternoon in Irving's office when he sat with Irving and me, squirming as he told a tale of woe. He was in the throes of being blackmailed by a mittel-European *femme fatale* with whom he'd had a whirl on a trip home to Berlin. But she had trailed Ernst back to Hollywood and was threatening to publish some letters he'd written her, unless he came through with fifty thousand of his hard-earned dollars.

Looking at him quizzically, Irving asked, "And what's *in* those letters?" Ernst sheepishly handed them over. After reading a line or two, Irving gave them back. "Look my friend," said he, "if you can keep *these* out of print for fifty thousand, you've got a bargain. Grab it!" So that smart European man of the world paid up like any American square.

Charlie Chaplin, Lubitsch,
Mary Pickford, and Douglas Fairbanks.

H.G. Wells loved to visit Hollywood.
He even liked to pose for the
studio cameras.

ometimes H.G. Wells took Paulette
d me out to a movie premiere.

H. G. Wells

Long before Hollywood became an
international tourist attraction, H.G.
Wells used to visit there. H.G. upset
the film colony's hosts and hostesses no
end because they never knew what
to talk about to such a higbrow. But
H.G. never fazed Paulette or me
because he had an insatiable appetite
for movie gossip, of which we always
had a fresh supply. Moreover, he never
avoided the news cameras of the
day and genuinely enjoyed being
photographed with Hollywood girls
like us.

217

To Darling
Anita
love from Cecil

Cecil Beaton really belongs in Edwardian Times, an era which he has re-created at his country house in rural England.

I've had fun collaborating on a new musical with Ralph Blane and Jim Gregory. While most lyricists grow hysterical on Tin Pan Alley, Ralph (whose hits include Judy Garland's "Trolley Song") retains his cool by living in his hometown, Broken Arrow, Oklahoma.

Henry Sell

The hometown of my choice is a party-giving community. New York will give a party for any reason, anytime, anyplace. The publication of a new book is always an excuse; but in 1974, when Henry Sell and Gerry Stutz joined forces to give a party for the publication of *Kiss Hollywood Good-by,* there was a problem: where to find a room big enough for all those guests. It was solved when Gerry offered her entire department store for the occasion.

Gerry is famous for being New York's most liberated store manager. Single-handedly, she turned the conservative old dress shop on West Fifty-Seventh known as Bendel's into the equivalent of a general store.

Just as Charles Dana Gibson created the belle of the Gay Nineties and John Held the Twenties' flapper, Gerry has created mannikins for her windows that epitomize the tall, rangy, liberated beauty of the Seventies, with the long mane of hair, just like a boy's.

The party was a success and an occasion for much sentiment. It had been Henry Sell who, fifty years before, had suggested extending my little story about Lorelei Lee with adventures abroad. If it had not been for Henry's suggestion . . .

Henry Sell helped Gerry Stutz give a party to celebrate the publication of my new book.

John Emerson

Sometimes I get enquiries concerning my marriage to a man who treated me with complete lack of consideration, tried to take credit for my work and appropriated all my earnings. Recently I got a letter from a certain Mr. Poe in which he asks, "Why did you submit for so many years to a husband who had so few redeeming qualities?"

The main reason is that my husband liberated me; granted me full freedom to choose my own companions. In most respects my freedom resembled that of Eliza Doolittle's in Bernard Shaw's *Pygmalion*, whose father generously gave her the whole, wide, blooming world in which to hustle. But my situation was a great deal better than Eliza's because the world in which my husband allowed me to roam was so delectable.

Before I met John Emerson, he had starred on Broadway in a play called *The Conspiracy,* in which he played an eccentric old detective. After meeting John, I was inspired to paint his portrait in that role. It was my first and last work of art, for it served my purpose of impressing a potential husband. Actually, almost every move I ever made was motivated by s-e-x.

Had he so desired, my husband could have imprisoned me; and, because I am a schnook by nature, I wouldn't have complained. I was too busy to give heed to being gypped; and all the while, my keep was being paid for in very luxurious locales. I thought that my husband's companions were uninspiring but he was only too happy to keep them to himself. I might have accused John of ingratitude, but I've always thought gratitude a rather smarmy virtue. Anyway, my husband's shenanigans made him a figure of fun; and so, torn between laughter and resentment, I opted for laughter.

I was so inexperienced when I first met John that, mistaking his male chauvinism for strength of character, I fell in love. As a wife I came to know better. There were times when I considered walking out on my marriage, but it would have left poor John without his base of operations.

My husband wept at the thought of being left alone, causing me feelings of guilt. The life he had chosen seemed so unrewarding, whereas mine was so consistently filled with excitement.

Nobody could hate John Emerson any more than one could hate Eliza Doolittle's pa. I honestly liked John, because, along the lines laid down by Will Rogers, I've never known a *man* I couldn't like.

And so, dear Mr. Poe, I hope your concern about this major mystery will return, like that famous Raven, nevermore.

George Cukor

George Cukor was ready to start directing *The Women* at M.G.M. when he was suddenly balked by a Board of Censors that removed the best jokes from Clare Luce's script. There was no time to write a new script, so George and I had to concoct each scene right there on the set just before the cameras started to grind.

In 1975, George Cukor returned from Leningrad, where he had accomplished the colossal task of directing Maeterlinck's *Bluebird* with a Russo-American cast. His New York friends gathered to celebrate George's return; among them the famed French farceur, Pierre Barillet, and A.L.

Rouben Mamoulian

Rouben Mamoulian is one of the first Hollywood directors to pay attention to the "composition" of scenes and to develop a special palette for each color film, just as if he were a painter.

Rouben's wife, Azadia, is herself a fine painter; but, disdaining a professional career, she chooses to paint for her own entertainment.

One rather spooky incident concerning Rouben occurred at a Sunday lunch party in Santa Monica. Rouben found himself in an argument with Aldous Huxley about Aldous' favorite psychic, whose name was Lola.

Rouben had recently been asked by a Hollywood hostess to pick Lola up for a party, where she was to tell fortunes. Rouben obliged, appearing in a new car he had purchased that same day, one that Lola graciously admired. Then, when it came Rouben's turn to be "read" by Lola, she told him quite significantly that he would be purchasing a new car the next week. Rouben was appalled that she should think he'd buy himself another new car.

However, on his way home from that lunch, Rouben crashed into a truck and demolished the car. So he had to buy a new car on the very date that Lola had predicted.

Bacherdy

In *I am a Camera,* Christopher Isherwood was writing about decadence in Berlin while I was investigating blondes in other world capitols. Our paths crossed in Santa Monica where we lived for eighteen years as neighbors.

In Vienna, Franz Lehár and I occupied adjacent rooms at the Auresburg Sanitarium. I was there for a sinus operation; Franz for minor surgery, and we left the door open between us in order to collaborate on our symptoms. To us they were much more fascinating than *The Merry Widow* or *Gentlemen Prefer Blondes.*

With best regards to the charmant Mes Anita Loos!
Vienna 19th May 1922 Lehár

In Vienna, I met Adolf Loos, my cousin-by-remote-control. Adolf was a famous architect, and he had had a great deal to do with the modernization of Vienna.

Viscount D'Abernon bore a marked resemblance to King Edward VII, and for a very good reason—consanguinity. Rumor had it that one of Edward's many lady friends was a certain vaudeville actress.

Morton Gottlieb

I recently shared a notable experience with Morton Gottlieb, producer of the two biggest Broadway hits of this decade. It took place during an exhibition of Fauvist paintings at the Museum of Modern Art. Mortie and I had postponed going to see the pictures because the museum was hopelessly over-crowded. But, while we were waiting for that flurry of art lovers to dwindle, a phone call came from Lillian Gerard, who is on the staff of MOMA. "The gallery is closed on Wednesdays," said Lillian, "so how would you like to bring a few friends to look at the Fauvist pictures in peace and quiet?"

Our guests that Wednesday were Paulette Goddard, Andy Warhol, and Andrew Wyeth. On leaving the exhibit, we were over-awed and even a little bit groggy from those dazzling Fauvist colors. And then Paulette, who is accustomed to the best of everything in life, made a trenchant comment. "This has been the greatest luxury I've ever known!"

A close tie between Mortie and me lies in our habit of early rising. Mortie phones me every morning, and we catch up on our daily routines. There's a lot to say because Mortie's two latest hits, *Sleuth* and *Same Time Next Year,* are playing all over the world.

Mortie has made the great discovery that talent is more entertaining than scenery. Both his major hits are played in one single set by a cast of two. It almost seems as if economy should be the better part of show business.

Mortie Gottlieb and A.L. at MOMA.

231

8
IT'S
LIGHTER
THAN
YOU THINK

While I was writing *Kiss Hollywood Good-by*, it began to dawn on me that the things I learned during thirty years of working on those old movie scripts prepared me better than any formal education for the wide world I was to enter on leaving Hollywood.

At M.G.M. during the Thirties, we harbored the most distinguished tragedienne since Eleanora Duse. Yet I came to learn that America's major interest in Greta Garbo was that she wore size eleven shoes and wanted to be alone. I also found out that Clark Gable's earthshaking charisma seemed to be of less import than the unusual size of his ears.

On leaving the studios, I came to be a friend of the fabulous Elsie deWolfe, who established interior decorating as a recognized profession and brought about an international revolution in taste. Yet the fact that really captivated Elsie's public was that she could stand on her head. Elsie's influence may still linger on. Today isn't the whole world standing on its head?

One might feel that, at my age, I should look on life with more gravity. After all, I've been privileged to listen, firsthand, to some of the most profound thinkers of my day: Aldous and Julian Huxley, H. G. Wells, Bertrand Russell, Arnold Bennett, and H. L. Mencken, who were all beset by gloom over the condition the world had gotten into. Then why can't I view it with anything but amusement?

In my own career, I've found, just like Elsie, that nothing I've accomplished nor

En route to Switzerland to join Helen
Hayes for the international tribute
to Dr. Jonas Salk for his vaccine against
polio, I missed connections with
Helen because a Swiss airplane is
generally two hours early. Just as, in the
old days, a ship was generally late.

   On a trip in 1917 with Mrs. Conway
Tearle, wife of the British actor who
starred with Constance Talmadge in my
film play, *A Virtuous Vamp*, it took the
Berengaria nine days to get to Cherbourg.

the important people I've met have impressed anyone as much as the fact that I like to get up early in the morning. It has nothing to do with viewing the sunrise, breathing the fresh morning air, or listening to the birds chirp as they greet the dawn.

For some reason, which must relate either to the genes or enzymes, the human race seems to be divided into night-people and day-people. Although I was born and raised in show business, I always got to bed as early as possible and woke up automatically at 4 A.M. without an alarm clock. I just happen to be a day-person.

And now, as my days accumulate, they have disclosed another unusual fact. I'm getting on in age.

Recently an earnest T.V. moderator asked me for a hint on how to grow old gracefully. Now what a typical T.V. cliché that is; when the one thing on which I am an authority is how to grow old disgracefully. I've just gone through the embarrassment of having the paperback edition of my book barred from the shelves of supermarkets in Texas . . . yet! Not on account of its text, but because the cover depicts an enticing nude who provided Texas housewives with unfair competition. So Texas husbands are deprived of seeing that last pretty Hollywood blonde, driven out of the movies by the mystique of Barbra Streisand, hitchhiking away from Hollywood to escape the grim political miasma of Jane Fonda and Shirley MacLaine.

Last month, on my birthday, some columnist printed that I'm 83, but I'm sure that's a lie. I'm much older. I refuse to inform myself how much, having decided that if I knew I'd begin to feel as ancient as I really am. So I wake up every morning with a childlike fascination over all things great and small.

In the first place, I can never take for granted the euphoria produced by a cup of coffee. I'm grateful every day that it isn't banned as a drug, that I don't have to buy it from a pusher, that its cost is minimal and there's no need to increase the intake. I can count on its stimulation three-hundred-and-sixty-five mornings every year. And, thanks to the magic in a cup of coffee, I'm able to plunge into a whole day's cheerful thinking.

The first thing I contemplate is my Bible. Another good habit for which I take no credit. For nearly forty-five years, my life style has been dictated by my mentor, critic, and spiritual guide—Gladys Tipton Turner. When first she came to work for me, I—like every other member of the film-colony—began my day with the gossip-column of Louella Parsons. Gladys soon broke that habit and replaced Louella with the Scriptures. At first I accepted the replacement as a chore. But I soon realized there was as much lively action in the Gospels as in Louella's column. And, thanks to Gladys, my first thought on waking up is to find out what's going on that morning in the Bible.

My viewpoint on all reading matter is based on trying to be equally fair. It's quite acceptable to take delight in such scamps as Shakespeare's Richard III, Goethe's Mephistopheles, Thackeray's Becky Sharp, and Dickens' Fagan. Then why shouldn't we be grateful for a real-life Richard Nixon, not only for his astounding moral turpitude, but for a unique brand of comedy relief? Perhaps Nixon's declaration, "I am not a crook!" will in time take on an epic quality, like the statement of Louis XVI who, on the date which marked the Fall of the Bastille, wrote in his diary, "Nothing happened today."

All-consuming though Watergate has been, don't let us be misled that it stands alone. I came into the world in time for my childish ears to hear about the Teapot Dome Scandal, when members of our State Department accepted bribes for government oil reserves. Then came the financial blot on France of the Stavisky case, which has only recently been made into a lurid movie. I now wait with bated breath for the film version of England's Profumo scandal, starring, let's hope, Raquel Welch.

I can appreciate all those events for having banished tedium in dismal homes all over the world and provided animated talk in what might otherwise have been some pretty dull cocktail parties.

It's true that, in our time, we can't ignore a daily roster of major crimes, but in all justice, why not follow through on those atrocities, take into account that their victims are comparatively few—while those of us who daily escape murder, muggers, rapists, or bombs are legion? Moreover, what human experience can match the exhilaration of a reprieve? Today, the most humble citizen can enjoy the ecstasy of a reprieve just by waking up to realize he's not in jail.

The most deadening of all experience is boredom. But today one breathtaking event after another gallops by so quickly that nobody ever has to be bored. Just to read a newspaper or hear a voice of doom on television or radio is an experience that rivals Dante at his best.

Who would want to exchange the shock value of a thief in the Vice Presidency for a scarehead that merely stated: "Alice Roosevelt barred from smoking cigarette in public?"

One safeguard against boredom in my own case is that age has brought on semi-deafness. Attending the plays of Albee or Pinter, my ears escape the gloom of their one-dimensional content. So at the theater, I relax, sit back and enjoy an opportunity to meditate on other matters that make more sense: the comic strips of Al Capp and the Peanut contingent, or that splendid book on Eastern philosophy, *Zen and the Art of Archery.*

There was a time when my major diversion lay in fashion. Today I can be grateful for faulty sight which views these modern garments as a mere blur. The

APEDA 2
N.Y.

dresses of yesteryear took cognizance of the female frame. But even a clever dress designer like Halston doesn't fool me—I know why he invented his caftan syndrome. It's because a caftan can be run up cheaply in two seams on a sewing machine, whereas the Garment Workers' Union has outpriced hand tailoring until only the un-taxed rich can pay for it. But I don't mind that Halston is forced to charge more money for a caftan than Balenciaga did for hand labor, because I have two closets full of vintage dresses made of organic materials that will last as long as I do.

I can even see a ray of light in the

The best way to appear impressive was to copy a pose from Gloria Swanson, who is no taller than I am.

A very good aid to looking soulful was to borrow a hat from Norma Talmadge, who had just brought forth floods of tears in *Smilin' Through*.

Cecil Beaton shot these two fashion pictures at his London studio. It was there that Cecil invented the fantasies he used as backgrounds, turning his photos into works of art that have now become collectors' items.

My dress in Cecil's portrait (LEFT) came from Lucien Lelong and was of bottle green tulle. It was a masterpiece of restraint, and I greatly preferred it to a spangled number (OPPOSITE) a Seventh Avenue dress firm had given me to wear for publicity. But both Lelong and I were wrong, and Seventh Avenue was right. That gaudy number earned so much attention I finally realized that, next to diamonds, spangles are a girl's best friend.

242

Hats used to come to the rescue of a girl's ego. The best of them were imported from Paris, but they quickly found their way to Hollywood in the Twenties. And it was there I made a dear friend in the nationally famous Mr. John, who gave me a fashion hint I followed as long as a girl could wear hats without being démodé: "Look honey," said Mr. John, "always wear something with an upward sweep." So the feathers on all my hats extended skyward.

present high cost of living. For today, when the price of so many commodities has risen sky high, sex is cheaper than at any other point in history. During the timorous Twenties, a man had to provide his girl with an expensive hideaway in the form of a love nest, had to set up charge accounts for her in the best stores and deck her out in genuine diamonds that used to be a girl's best friend.

Today any man can get the same service for the cost of a martini in any neighborhood bar. (Sometimes a girl will even pay for the martini.) And, servants being a thing of the past, any male who wants to gamble on marriage can get a wife, mother-substitute, and servant girl all thrown in for free.

We can now enjoy other benefits that have never before existed. A minor new joy is to turn on television and, with a flick of the wrist, cause *The Beverly Hillbillies* to vanish, and—presto-chango—we have *The Ascent of Man*.

One very great advantage of these days is the fact that nobody has to be faulted for running out on obligations. The cult of Sigmund Freud has supplied derelicts with excuses to dodge responsibility by simply slumping onto a couch and being told they're sick.

In these troubled times, I take great comfort in the simple basic human equation, which is so ingrained in our very genes that it will always motivate behavior.

So no matter how hopeless things appear to be the human equation will provide our survival.

Let us take the case of that terribly dangerous political affiliation, when China followed Russia into communism. By sticking together, the two nations could easily have swallowed the entire world. But it is inherent in the human equation that allies quickly come to detest each other, and the split between those two powers has made our world much safer for democracy.

I have also found that the best way to face up to any problem in these difficult times is to follow the advice of my own private guide, Gladys, who states that the Bible describes just what happens to people who behave badly and spells out, sometimes in red ink, the advantages of good behavior. So that all anybody really needs to learn are two short words: behave yourself.

During the first two years of Douglas Fairbanks' career as a silent-movie star, I wrote his scripts. Our troupe lived and worked in a male-oriented group, of which I was the only female. Doug was a sort of amateur guru and, as such, used to encourage us to give way to impulses. "Exercise your emotions," Doug used to scold us. "Don't be clods! Put a little *life* into your living."

Doug followed his own advice; he never sat when he could stand, never walked when he could run; and, to Doug, chasms were built to jump over.

Doug Fairbanks could conquer any
living space.

Doug was never stopped by fear of
water. But a stunt I wrote in one of my
silent movies suddenly developed
an incredible cowardice in Doug; he
tried over and over to do the stunt
and finally said, "I can't do this scene,
Nita; I'm scared." The scene
required Doug to stick a hat-pin
into an automobile tire.

To go into technicalities, these excerpts are from my scripts for two silent movies—*His Picture in the Papers* and *A Virtuous Vamp.*

Selma

family

never me

His Picture in the Papers

A SELF-MADE MAN WHO ADORES HIS MAKER,

S. T.   PROTEUS PRINDLE, MANUFACTURER OF PRINDLE'S 27 VARIETIES OF VEGETARIAN FOOD PRODUCTS-- COUNT 'EM, "27".

1   PRINDLE'S OFFICE. Prindle showing and describing his various articles of food to a customer, and "pointing with pride".

S. T.   PEARL AND PANSY, PRINDLE'S DAUGHTERS, COMMONLY KNOWN AS "28" and "29" (Count 'em), PUSHING THE PRINDLE PRODUCTS.

2   PRINDLE'S DINING ROOM. Daughters feeding guests the various Prindle products, in course of giving a Tea Party.

S. T.   "PETE" PRINDLE, THE "NONCOMFORMIST MEMBER" OF THE FAMILY.

3   PRINDLE'S INNER OFFICE. Pete asleep at his desk- father comes in- wakes Pete- father shows displeasure at the slothfulness of Pete and tells him if he doesn't go to work he will disinherit him- Peter is a little worried and decides he will really go to work- squares his shoulders and opens desk compartment- takes out whiskey and seltzer and mixes himself a highball and puts it on his desk- adjusts electric fan- rings bell- stenographer enters and sits to take dictation- phone rings- stenographer answers it and announces Miss Vera Kercove- he talks over the phone.

4   VERA'S OFFICE. Vera talking at phone, pleasantly. Other girls with her, laughing.

5   PRINDLE'S INNER OFFICE. Pete finishes talking and hangs up phone- dismisses his stenographer- hides the booze- puts on his hat and sneaks out.

-1-

FORM 112 10M CITIZEN

Date...............

No. ....

Please return to Script Dept.

METRO-GOLDWYN-MAYER
STUDIOS

Culver City, Calif.   1380

A VIRTUOUS VAMP

Screen Story
by
Anita Loos
and
John Emerson

of her eye, indulges in a little smile to

herself at the idea of their boasting of their

family, then turns to them and quizzically says:

SP.   "DO YOU KNOW ANYTHING AGAINST MY FAMILY?"

The sisters shrug their shoulders, give her

another look up and down, and then turn to

each other and then one of them says of course

they have no doubt her family is a perfectly

respectable one -

SP.   "BUT IT IS OBVIOUS, MISS JONES, YOU ARE NOT OF OUR
            CLASS."

Gwen now begins to boil inwardly at these

insults and the unspeakable snobbery of these

women. She is almost on the verge of telling

them where they get off, who she is and what

she thinks of them but she suppresses this in-

clination and says to them:

SP.   "WHEN I MARRY YOUR BROTHER, I MARRY HIM AND NOT
            HIS FAMILY."

The sisters try to think of further argument

but they are at the end of their resources so

far as persuasion goes. They look at each

other and decide to change their tactics. One

of them comes to Gwen and says that she must

realize this is a misalliance, that it would

not mean happiness to either party, that she

of course understands the great advantage it

would be to Gwen in a financial way and says:

SP.   "IF YOU WILL RENOUNCE THE ENGAGEMENT, WE WILL GLADLY
            PAY YOU ANY REASONABLE AMOUNT."

Doug's thinking, however, was purely second-hand; he was repeating the philosophy of his idol, Theodore Roosevelt, whose main precept was to "speak softly but carry a big stick." But to speak softly is pointless unless one's words have clout. It was Teddy Roosevelt who formed the character of his daughter Alice who, today in her nineties, is the most exciting female in a world that produced Elizabeth Taylor and Raquel Welch.

Doug's teaching took its most notable effect on me when, early in the Twenties, I cut off my hair. At that time, such a move was even more radical than for a girl to lose her virginity. The latter could be hidden, but bobbed hair was a stigma for all to see, and a girl who shortened her hair was supposed to destroy her sex appeal.

Women were stupid not to have recognized the fact that George Sand, in dispensing with the corkscrew curls of *her* era, had gone on to annex the most erotic collection of lovers in her century. But her short hair so shocked an unthinking womankind that they never tried to copy it; George didn't create a cult or launch a fashion.

In the days of my youth, girls were the victims of a bulky hairdo termed the "marcel wave." They sat for long stretches in beauty parlors, having their hair tortured into a cast iron semblance of ocean waves. I had an abundance of long hair that could take the fashion in stride. It was also a matter of pride to my mother, who would make me take out the hairpins and show off its length. I knew better; the best feature I owned was the compact proportion of my head. And the only way to show it off was to get rid of those marcel waves.

Such a desecration, however, would never have been allowed under the same roof with my mother. I had to get away from home to commit it. The moment of liberation came when I was offered a trip to New York in the entourage of D. W. Griffith.

I had never set foot outside the boundaries of California, and New York had been a Paradise in my best dreams. The lifestyle of Hollywood was based on its films, and I found it spurious. A waitress in Hollywood had no interest in serving at table; she was waiting for Darryl Zanuck to show up and promote her to stardom. A Hollywood taxi driver was always on the lookout for a chance to pick up Jack Warner. But away from the blight of films, waitresses and taxi drivers could enjoy endless dimensions for "putting a little *real* life into their living." And, in the vast population of New York, a girl could find every type of individual she craved.

Now, in my choice of reading matter, I was obsessed by the editorials written by H. L. Mencken in *Smart Set* magazine. I had been tempted to write Mencken a fan letter, addressed to his office in New York, but my experience in studios had given fan mail a bad name. And now I was on the verge of breathing the same

Too much hair can smother a girl's ego.

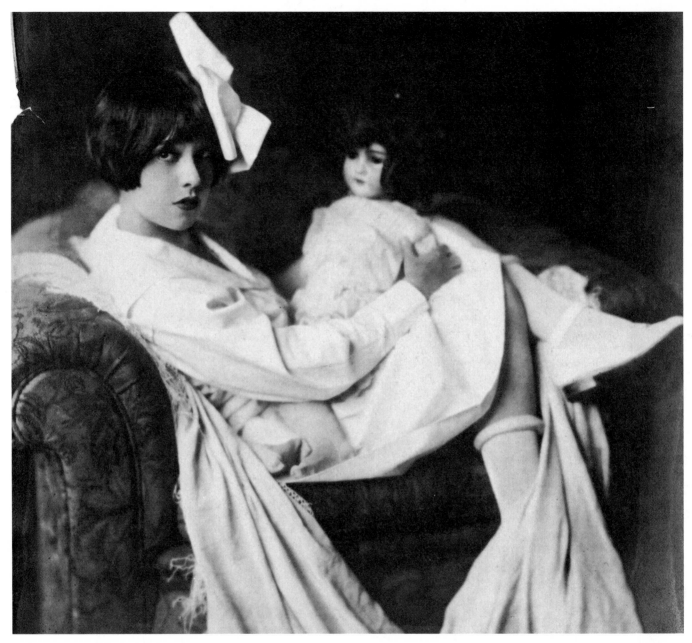

At a New York costume party long after I had become a seasoned matron.

In black velvet with a white flannel collar, from Gabrielle Chanel. She would talk to me non-stop, but her only subject was Chanel. I've come to forgive Coco's egomania through a recent memoir by Paul Morand, in which she confessed to chattering endlessly because, if she stopped, she might be overlooked. Actually, the great Chanel was insecure.

250

251

New York air as Henry Mencken.

But, first of all, my personality had to be released. No sooner had the Griffith troupe checked into the Algonquin Hotel than I phoned down to the barber shop for an appointment. The barber apparently thought I was a secretary phoning for my boss, because when I appeared and explained what I had in mind, he was appalled. "Does your mother know about this?" he asked. Ducking out on the truth, I evasively said she was in Hollywood. "Then you'd better go home and ask some Hollywood barber to do the job," said he. But, seeing my disappointment he finally added, "Tell you what I'll do. I'll lend you my scissors and you can go to your room and do it yourself. But don't blame me for the result!"

I took him up on it. The job required some contortions, but I managed it. And, when I returned the scissors, he consented, although visibly shaken, to trim off the ragged ends. Rising above those marcel waves, I sensed a complete liberation.

Now the subject of hair, which may seem so frivolous, is much more than a matter of vanity; it has an impact that is downright cosmic. We are all born with genes and chromosomes that regulate our egos, willy-nilly, and make us irretrievably what we are. But the Creator, in His infinite mercy, has given us hair with which we can do anything we like. We can grow it long, cut it short, straighten, crimp, tease, dye, or bleach it, and change the basics of our very lives. Hair can direct our future, dominate our present, make us look back in anger, or in gratitude, to our past. And it can regulate the degree of our triumphs or defeats.

Even so, it took some time for the shock of my first windblown bob to wear off. I still have a letter from a beau, Tommy Smith (the same Tommy who was later to publish the first edition of *G.P.B.* as a sort of outsized Christmas card). Tommy had had to take a trip abroad, and when we said goodbye, he asked me to send him a photograph to Vienna, which I did. His thank you note reads:

Dearest Anita:

I cannot tell you how happy for a moment, but also how very sad upon further contemplation, your photograph made me. Here was a lovely creature with the manner, conversation and gait of one of the wickedest tomboys I have ever known. But the hair—what can I say about that? God help us when our best bad girls are changing!

Never-the-less, love always,
Tommy

It was by pure accident that I stumbled onto the importance of blonde hair as an aphrodisiac. I had no idea of any sexual economics underlying the bedtime successes of my heroine. At the same time, I *did* realize that her thriftless brunette girl friend had a great deal of fun while my successful blonde stagnated.

There always has to be a psychological letdown in successful gold digging. Inwardly a girl has got to realize, "This man is inferior, because he knows he has to pay for sex." And where can there be true satisfaction in hooking any second-rater?

This trait in us females has been put to good use by the truly great lovers of the world—the Don Juans, the Rubirosas, and the Aly Khans—none of whom ever gave any girl a gift commensurate with his means.

The most powerful love affairs share that same generous premise. Cleopatra took on Mark Antony and his entire Roman army as house guests of Egypt. The Queen of Sheba provided Solomon with luxuries that, even as a King, he couldn't afford. Psalms like "The Song of Songs" will never be written to a gold digger. There was an endearing spokeswoman for that subject in Fanny Brice, whose song in praise of giving was called "My Man," and it invested any girl's sexual *largesse* with a poignant ecstasy.

I began quite early in life to sense the thrill a girl attains in supplying money to a man. Gladys (who always knows whereof she speaks) summed up my philosophy in a simple aphorism one day, when in announcing a phone call from an Argentinian gigolo she said, "Miss Loos, you sure are flypaper for pimps!"

There is no better gauge of the humanities than a nation's popular songs. In "Yankee Doodle" a new country kicked up its heels in celebration of freedom. "Home Sweet Home" glorified a situation when domesticity was pleasant. "Old Black Joe" mourned the end of unpaid colored labor. Today we suffer a gaggle of rock ditties of which nobody has yet heard the lyrics, because they're drowned by noise.

But there now comes a truly stimulating ballad which has all the piercing sweetness of abnegation. The fact that "Tie a Yellow Ribbon Round the Old Oak Tree" has so instantly become a standard, makes it a sort of anchor to hope for our return to a more brisk sexual satisfaction in the future.

The song concerns a jailbird, just released from a stretch for a crime of which he was guilty. Jail has supplied him with only a small amount of severance money, and he has nothing else to depend on . . . except the sweetheart whom he wronged. An honest move would have been to phone her and say, "Mamma, can I come back?" But our hero sensed it would be too easy a reflex for her to slam down the receiver.

So, with the exquisite poesy of a born pimp, he sends her the following message: "You can tie a yellow ribbon round the old oak tree, if you still want me . . . if you still want me." And if, when he nears her front yard, the oak

253

tree bears no yellow ribbon, he'll "stay on the bus, forget about us, and put the blame on me."

So the lady has the choice of dumping him, as any Gloria Steinem would—or she can tie that ribbon on the oak tree and be exquisitely hooked until he leaves her or gets busted again.

But the lady of the song chooses defeat; a choice so thrilling, not only to her, but to all the other passengers on the bus, that they rise in unison to cheer

Lillian Gish can be angelic both on-screen and off.

that bolt of yellow ribbon from the local Woolworth's.

Intelligence in a female can only be an asset to sex if it is well disguised. In the past generation, the women most widely acclaimed for brains have been Janet Flanner, Lillian Hellman, and Dorothy Parker; the two latter had unsatisfactory relationships with men; the former was too smart to get involved. One girl who succeeded in spite of her brains was the Duchess of Windsor. But she sugar-coated her mentality with Southern charm and a devotion to amenities, most of which are foolish, except for her appreciation of gourmet cookery.

I once had a demonstration of being brainless when I visited Germany and didn't know a word of German. In Vienna, I met a very chic type who proceeded to escort me around and took me one evening to the Sacher Hotel for dinner. It was there that the climax of our romance took place when he helped me cut up my apple strudel. But I later learned enough German to express my thoughts, at which he disappeared like mist from the River Rhine.

In *Gentlemen Prefer Blondes* I quoted an observation made by one of the greatest sirens I've ever known, who declared, "I think that bird-life is the highest form of civilization." Today in her seventies, Lillian Gish is still the same blonde idol to men that she was in her teens. She won the adoration of D.W. Griffith to the neglect of a heady sexpot

When Fanny Brice torched for that man of hers, she had to substitute the fascinating rascal with a cold impersonal lamp-post.

named Norma Talmadge. Lillian so influenced the Master's libido that he chose every star he ever directed by her ability to imitate Lillian's mannerisms; the provocative fluttering about, and the innocent batting of eyelids. Most likely her virginal state is responsible for D. W.'s films retaining their allure in this age of instant fornication.

Like the "weather" of Mark Twain's great aphorism, everybody talks about sex.

When first I knew Bill Faulkner, he was partial to pure, crystal-clear, moonshine whiskey.

But nobody ever does the right thing about it. Today people relate sexual satisfaction to such non-sequiturs as psychoanalysis, pills, drugs, hallucinogenics, Yoga, diet, and the permissiveness of college campuses.

Only now do I myself begin to realize that all the important moves I ever made were guided by men; any lessons of lasting value were taught, outside of school, by men who were definitely not professors.

My small book has now passed on, as a period piece, to the great-grandchildren of its first readers. And may they learn a lesson from the male-dominated Dorothy who never owned a diamond, but had a great deal more joy from the love-token of a bangle.

Soon after the publication of *G.P.B.*, I received a fan letter that states:
You have played a rotten trick on your public. How many of them, do you think, will ever know that your scatter-brained Dorothy has something; that the dancing man, le gigolo, was really somebody? Have you perhaps builded better than you knew?

His letter ends with:

I wish I had thought of Dorothy first.
                                    Sincerely,
                                    William Faulkner
New Orleans
Febry 1926

In the long run a brunette may enjoy

256

Ste Claire du Château
Hyères . — Jan 12 . 26 .

So many thanks for
your card, & best greetings
for the New Year. —
We are just reading
the Great American
Novel (at last!) "Gentle-

POST CARD
CARTE POSTALE
Communication—Correspondance
Address—Adresse
STAMP
HERE

men Prefer Blondes", & I want to
know if there are — or will be —
others, & if you know the young
woman, who must be a genius —
All my good wishes for
1926.
Edith Wharton

TWENTIETH CENTURY
PICTURES Inc.
1041 No. Formosa - Hollywood - California

OFFICE OF
JOSEPH M. SCHENCK
PRESIDENT

Dear Anita
From your ardent admirer
who never had a chance
to be more than that but
is still living in hope
Joe

Like I said, I could
have been in movies.

Edith Wharton wrote
of *G.P.B.* on a
postcard, "at last—
the great American
novel!"

257

certain other triumphs. The very gentleman who had once overlooked me in preference for a blonde, appeared to have had second thoughts. He ultimately wrote me a mash note in the vernacular of Lorelei Lee herself, and it reads as follows:

H. L. MENCKEN
1524 HOLLINS ST.
BALTIMORE
December 29th

Dear Miss Anita:-
Well, a woman with a husband who lolls around with actresses and has his picture taken showing him smirking at them with his necktie half way around to his ear certainly deserves to be allowed to take a look herself at a handsome man once in a while and if she sends him a pitcher of herself and he gets mashed on it then certainly no one has got any call to remark on it so long as he behaves like a gentleman and don't call her up and try to get her to make a date with him in some tea-room or other where all you can see is a lot of women that ought to be home getting their husbands' meals sitting there with a lot of bums wasting their time.

Mit evangelischem Gruss

The Bavarian costume is superb. It makes me yodel.

After waiting many years for that last laugh on a blonde, I finally began to chuckle.

Private Collection

With a nature as gloomy as his name,
Billy Grimm could only see me as
a sad Roumanian.

I own pictures by such masters as
Renoir, Rouault, Toulouse-Lautrec,
Modigliani, and sketches by Rodin of
models for his sculptures. All these have
their snob appeal, but the paintings that
have really registered with me are by
friends.

To an Austrian artist, I had the
weltschmerz of a downhearted
Viennese frail.

A portrait by Federico Pallavicini
featured a dress by Lanvin. Federico
had also drawn the illustrations
for *A Mouse Is Born,* which is my own
favorite among all the books I've
written.

Sketched in the 1950s by René
Bouché, who was the fashionable
painter for New York society, as well
a great portraitist of Broadway.
Many of his works are owned by the
Museum of the City of New York.

I never ceased being a model for Cecil Beaton. Early in our friendship, he had painted me in Vienna, wearing an Austrian leather jacket. I envy the girl Cecil saw because she seems to have a certain innocence.

During the Fifties in New York, Cecil again drew me and indicated that my girlish innocence had turned into a sort of amused resignation.

This portrait by Doug Davis wrings my heart. Doug, who was Edith Piaf's last lover, was killed in a massive plane crash at Le Bourget airport in Paris. Doug left me a painting that later decorated the book jacket of *A Girl Like I.*

I have often been painted by Don Bachardy, but my favorite is the one in which I wear a hat, a piece of apparel that is almost extinct today.

These fashions of yesteryear were designed for me by a master—Mainbocher. At that time, Main was the foremost couturier of Paris. Among his clients was the Duchess of Windsor, for whom Main created a wedding gown that became historic. It was copied by Seventh Avenue and worn by purchasers of every age and weight, from Miami, Florida, to Anchorage, Alaska.

Model T-56

Black lace veil - Black bows. Lace scarf to throw
over chin - or across back.
Very charming -
choice for you -

Model T-65

Red ostrich feather -
tiny black velvet bows -
worn very far forward
on brow - chic & trendy chic.

Model T-59

Black ostrich
with 2 fancies -
also worn forward
slightly to side
of forehead

Model T-66

Three black ostrich
worn slightly to side
and far over forehead -
bows is of satin in
either black or red.
My 3rd choice for you.

Model T-64

Black ostrich
Butterflies - This
I feel would be
perfect for you. Small
lace veil if you care

FOR :—

MISS ANITA LOOS.

During the Fifties, I visited the exhibition of Marcel Proust's memorabilia in Paris. I found that his manuscripts were as messy as mine. What a thrill—to have even a defect in common with the great master.

One day, Colette invited me to bring an artist friend for tea. We found the great lady sound asleep on the *chaise longue* in her salon. My friend happened to have brought along his painting kit, so he sat down and quietly sketched Colette. She never woke up, and finally we tiptoed out without our tea.

to Anita from
Mogens Turde

Colette
M.T.

"Pretend you don't notice them."

Peter Arno sent me this, but there is
an important message on the other side
that can't be seen. Peter wrote,
"To Anita, with great love."

This sketch of Emmet Kelly's was
made on the spot in Saratoga, while I
was visiting John Ringling North
in the winter quarters of his circus.

In Dublin one summer, I ran into Jack Yeats, the brother of the great Irish poet. He asked me to his studio, where he showed me a picture he'd been inspired to paint after reading *G.P.B.* The title of Jack's painting is "Gentlemen Prefer *Books*," and it touched me because his model for the gentleman in the picture happened to be my dear friend Ernest Boyd, the Irish essayist. I eagerly paid Jack $250 for his painting, and have recently turned down ten times that sum for sentimental reasons. In appearance, Ernest Boyd resembled the portraits of our Saviour, and he once wrote on a photograph to me, "What a friend you have in Jesus."

270

Catching Up With Anita Loos, or How Times Have Changed

By ISRAEL SHENKER

①
"I put birthdays out of my mind as far as I can," said Anita Loos, the author, trying to forget that today's birthday is her 80th.

"Books always give me the wrong age, and I'm sure I'm older than they say. The two biggest bores I ever met were Maurice Chevalier and Lady Mendl, and they did nothing but worry about their age.

tions organization. She certainly wouldn't have any champagne: there wouldn't be time for it. She'd have to get to her job by 9, 9:30.

"I can't wait to get to my desk each morning. As soon as I found out there was money in ink I dropped acting and stocked up on ink. I tried a typewriter, but it was uncomfortable. I'm 4 feet 11 and I weigh 94 pounds.

②

LETTERS OF JAMES JOYCE (437 pp.)—
Edited by Stuart Gilbert—Viking ($7.50)

James Joyce, the great artificer of words who both revitalized and nearly destroyed the English novel with *Ulysses* and left even some of his admire~ and in the labyrinth of *Fi~* not be remem~ them ~

③
H
of ~
Fro~

everywhere.' " When he was eyesight he devoted hours to rea~ after two pages of a book abou~ *tlemen Prefer Blondes*, but lost ~ Lawrence's sex-ridden *Lady Cha~ Lover.* The critique was, he tho~ piece of propaganda "in favou~ thing which, outside of ~ country at any rate, makes a ~ ganda for itself."

⑥
Ireland was in his veins. H~ of his life on the Continent, ~ Paris, Zurich, but his writing ~ Dublin. His maturity was sp~ the first 22 years of his life on ~ infusing them with the thousan~ ~hat h~

④
MISS ANITA LOOS is unique; there never has been anything like her before, there never will be again; she is an amazing specimen, so absolutely of her time, a cute little Venus that only twentieth-century New York could have produced, a pocket Venus with a perfectly proportioned body on a Lilliputian scale, with a waist measurement of twenty inches and a hip measur~ent of thirty, with feet and legs that are up~ ~utive. She is the most delica~ with her pursed lips and spring~ pretty but sufficiently barb~ all sculptors, with her hard~ wicked, little Mongolian bead~ mouth. It is a mouth th~ perfect laugh: very few mo~ well, but her laugh is a ~ Here, indeed, is a new st~

⑤
Subliminal Graffiti
It is plain that the subconscious is a wicked witch's br~ of superhuman interest for all boys and girls. This *Mona L~* affair raises a major aspect of Professor Key's study. Do~ the discovery of graffiti in the deodorants and aids to glamo~ threaten the public of consumers, or does it merely reve~ the childish itch of the admen themselves? For example, th~ title *Gentlemen Prefer Blondes* may be both immoral and ~ immortal because it links hair and gold, faces and feces. Fo~ gold and dung have always had affinities, even as the greatest ~ perfumes include a subtle ingredient of excrement.

There is the further fetching factor of the author's name, ~ Anita Loos. It doesn't suggest the prim Puritan altogether. ~ Since the world of dung and excrement is quite near to the~ daily conscious level, are we to panic when the admen put~ ~hese at the bottom of the big hamper of goodies that they ~ ~roffer the affluent?

Will the graffiti hidd~

⑧
A high point for Edith Wharton in the winter of 1926 was reading *Gentlemen Prefer Blondes* by Anita Loos, "which the literary committee of Ste. Claire (R. Norton, G. Lapsley and EW) unhesitatingly pronounce the greatest novel since *Manon Lescaut*." Edith was only slightly exaggerating her response to this popular gem of American literary humor. In the same letter, to Hugh Smith, she spoke deprecatingly of Proust's recent *Albertine disparue:* "Walter calls it 'Proust disparu,' and he's nearly right." She allowed herself to be quoted as saying that Miss Loos's book "is *the* great American novel." This unmodified comment was flanked in advertisements by James Joyce's remark that he was putting *Gentlemen Prefer Blondes* "in place of honor" and George Santayana's solemn contention that it was unquestionably "the best book on philosophy written by an American."

Gentlemen Prefer Blondes consists of the diary ruminations of Lorelei Lee, a cheerfully amoral and dim-witted young woman from Little Rock, who, after shooting her employer for trying to entice her into a nasty situation, beats her way across the Atlantic and across England and the continent, engaging in a serie~ of dalliances and intrigues. Edith probably saw in the novel a deft satirical twis~ on her own satirical comedies of manners, as Lorelei, moving from one Ritz Hot~ to another, mixes with American tourists, British baronets, and French solicito~ and makes vague stabs at improving her mind by reading Conrad and Benvenu~ Cellini. The heroine's rushingly incoherent speech and phonetic spelling a~ attracted her. The characterization of Undine Spragg in *The Custom of ~* ~ Edith thought, was now vindicated.

~~ at *Vanity Fair*, a word of praise for ~ ~time sen~

⑨
THE EVER-PRESENT PAST
for the ironies of life. We could enjoy him as ~ twentieth-century Jane Austen if he would only ~ universe alone and learn to laugh at himself. W~ we not have lost if Miss Austen had been unable ~ if she had persisted in holding up Mr. Collins to ~ Christian Church, and Mr. Wickham to damn a~ Schnitzler's Anatol and Max can match any of Mr~ way's bad young men, but Schnitzler takes them ~ they are, not as an argument of despair for ma~ that book of balance and proportion, *Gentlem~ Blondes*, Miss Anita Loos does not bring an i~ against the universe in the person of Lorelei. S~ how to laugh, and that knowledge is the very bes~ tive there is against losing the true perspective ~ young men beware. Without a sense of humor ~ keep hands off the universe unless one is prepa~ oneself an unconscious addition to the sum of the ~

Through Rose-Colored Glasses

SMOND left. Aldous and Maria went off on
r journeys—three weeks, five thousand miles,
nal parks in the vast American Northwest.
e, Idaho, they sent a postcard to Anita Loos.

here was a young lady of Bute
ho was so indescribably cute
    That, each time she came out,
    All the boys gave a shout,
ith the Lesbians hot in pursuit.

Love Aldous

ne add!! M.

was another whose looks seemed surprisingly
ke her heroine in *Gentlemen Prefer Blondes*, Miss
ce has gone into the annals of American history.
ung girl of Pocket Edition proportions, she found
advantage when it came to choosing clothes for
early photographs, with the black, shining hair
y coils, she seems to be overwhelmed by the draped
d sealskin, the voluminous coats, skirts, stoles, and
t moving-picture era. But with the twenties, Anita
her own. The new fashions gave her the
erself. She cut her hair as short as that o
d went off to buy her hats and dress
nents of the great stores. Dressed as cr
child at the outset of an expedition can
l fringe meticulously combed, her buc
hool satchel, her Buster Brown hats and
os became the embodiment of cuteness.
wn grammar and syntax of fashion; an
er s

(7) Anita Loos and Sexual Economics:
"Gentlemen Prefer Blondes"
T. E. BLOM

In January, 1926, Edith Wharton wrote Frank Crowninshield that she was "just reading the Great American novel (*at last!*) 'Gentlemen Prefer Blondes,' & I want to know if there are – or will be – others, & if you knew the funny woman, who must be a genius –." Crowninshield did indeed know Anita Loos; he sent Wharton's postcard to her, and when Loos suggested to Wharton that she had overpraised the book, Wharton responded: "I meant every word I wrote about 'Blondes.'"[1] In February of the same year, William Faulkner wrote Loos,

I have just read the Blonde book. … Please accept my envious congratulations on Dorothy –
her through the (intelligence?) of that elegant moron of a cornflower. Only
miring public. How many of them, do you think,
n le gigolo, was really

THE NEW YORKER

(10) PROFILES
THE CHILD WONDER

WHEN the first instalment of Anita Loos' "Gentlemen Prefer Blondes" appeared in *Harper's Bazar*, there were ahead of the book many of the unexpected and capricious perils that so often beset the birth of a masterpiece, but it rose to its present enormous success under that same mysterious star of destiny that has guided Anita Loos with unfailing steadfastness throughout her brilliant ascent from stage child in a San Diego stock company to a place among the first humorists of the land. Indeed any biogra

her with fals
views her vast
with a kind of
believing in it
partly due to
self-critic, whi
over-rated, and
invincible shyne
to be lionized o
summer, all Eu
The stage was se

Hollywood; her
second book abo

(11) They crossed the continent by train, spent a few days in Chicago, went on to New York. If there was one person Aldous wanted to meet, it was Miss Anita Loos. He adored *Gentlemen Prefer Blondes*. He wrote her a fan letter.

. . I was enraptured by the book, have just hugely enjoyed the play, and am to be in America so short a time that I have no leisure to do things in the polite and tortuous way . . .

Also by Anita Loos

Novels

Gentlemen Prefer Blondes (1925)
But They Marry Brunettes (1927)
A Mouse Is Born (1951)
No Mother to Guide Her (1961)

Non-Fiction

A Girl Like I (1966)
Twice Over Lightly (with Helen Hayes, 1972)
Kiss Hollywood Good-by (1974)

Plays

The Whole Town's Talking (with John Emerson, 1923)
The Fall of Eve (with John Emerson, 1925)
Gentlemen Prefer Blondes (with John Emerson, 1926)
The Social Register (with John Emerson, 1931)
Happy Birthday (1946)
Gigi (adapted from the novel by Colette, 1951)
Chéri (adapted from the novel by Colette, 1959)
The King's Mare (adapted from the French of Jean Canolle; London, 1966)
Siegfried (adapted from the French of Jean Giraudoux, 1949)
Mrs. Smarty Gives a Party (adapted from the French of Pierre Barillet and Jean-Pierre Gredy, 1970)

Musicals

Gentlemen Prefer Blondes (music by Jule Styne, lyrics by Leo Robin, 1951)
Gogo Loves You (music by Claude Leveillee, lyrics by Gladys Shelley, 1964)
Lorelei (based on *Gentlemen Prefer Blondes*, with additional music by Jule Styne and lyrics by Betty Comden and Adolph Green, 1974)
All about Anne (with music and lyrics by Ralph Blane and James Gregory)
Happy Birthday (with music by Gerry Mulligan, lyrics by Judy Holiday)

Screenplays

The Power of the Camera (1912)
The Road to Plaindale (1912)
The New York Hat (1912)

He Was a College Boy (1912)
The Earl and the Tomboy (1912)
A Horse on Bill (1913)
A Hicksville Epicure (1913)
Highbrow Love (1913)
A Hicksville Romance (1913)
A Fallen Hero (1913)
A Fireman's Love (1913)
A Cure for Suffragettes (1913)
The Suicide Pact (1913)
Binks Runs Away (1913)
How the Day Was Saved (1913)
When a Woman Guides (1913)
Fall of Hicksville's Finest (1913)
The Wedding Gown (1913)
Yiddish Love (1913)
Gentlemen and Thieves (1913)
A Bunch of Flowers (1913)
Pa Says (1913)
The Widow's Kids (1913)
The Lady in Black (1913)
The Deacon's Whiskers (1913)
His Awful Vengeance (1913)
All for Mabel (1913)
The Fatal Deception (1913)
For Her Father's Sins (1913)
Unlucky Jim (1913)
All on Account of a Cold (1913)
The Saving Grace (1913)
A Narrow Escape (1913)
Two Women (1913)
The Wall Flower (1913)
Queen of the Carnival (1913)
The Mayor Elect (1913)
The Making of a Masher (1913)
Path of True Love (1913)
A Girl Like Mother (1913)
The Mother (1913)
The Great Motor Race (1913)
His Hoodoo (1913)
The Meal Ticket (1914)
The Saving Presence (1914)
The Suffering of Susan (1914)
The Chieftain's Daughter (Some Bull's Daughter, 1914)
The Fatal Dress Suit (1914)
The Girl in the Shack (1914)
The Saving Presence (1914)
His Hated Rival (1914)
A Corner in Hats (1914)
Nearly a Burglar's Bride (1914)

The Fatal Curve (1914)
The Million-Dollar Bride (1914)
A Flurry in Art (1914)
Nellie, the Female Villain (1914)
His Rival (1914)
Where the Roads Part (1914)
A No Bull Spy (1914)
A Balked Heredity (1914)
A Blasted Romance (1914)
Mortimer's Millions (1914)
A Life and Death Affair (1914)
The Sensible Girl (1914)
At the Tunnel's End (1914)
The Deadly Glass of Beer (1914)
The Stolen Masterpiece (1914)
The Last Drink of Whiskey (1914)
Nell's Eugenic Wedding (1914)
The School of Acting (1914)
A Hicksville Reformer (1914)
The White Slave Catchers (1914)
The Style Accustomed (1914)
The Deceiver (1914)
How They Met (1914)
The Cost of a Bargain (1915)
Sympathy Sal (1915)
Nelly, the Female Victim (1915)
Mixed Values (1915)
Pennington's Choice (from a story by J.A.
    Culley, 1915)
The Tear on the Page (1915)
How to Keep a Husband (1915)
The Burlesquers (1915)
The Fatal Fourth (1915)
The Fatal Fingerprints (1915)
Wards of Fate (1915)
Heart that Truly Loved (1915)
The Little Liar (1915)
Mountain Bred (1915)
Macbeth (titles, 1916)
A Corner in Cotton (1916)
Wild Girl of the Sierras (with F.M. Pierson,
    1916)
Calico Vampire (1916)
Laundry Liz (1916)
French Milliner (1916)
The Wharf Rat (1916)
Stranded (1916)
The Social Secretary (1916)
His Picture in the Papers (1916)
The Half-Breed (based on "In the Carquinez
    Woods," by Bret Harte, 1916)

American Aristocracy (1916)
Manhattan Madness (1916)
The Matrimaniac (with John Emerson,
    1916)
Intolerance (titles, 1916)
The Americano (based on "Blaze
    Derringer," by Anita Loos, 1917)
In Again, Out Again (1917)
Wild and Woolly (based on a story by H.B.
    Carpenter, 1917)
Reaching for the Moon (with John Emerson,
    1917)
Down to Earth (based on a story by Douglas
    Fairbanks, 1917)
Let's Get a Divorce (with John Emerson,
    based on a play by Victorien Sardou,
    1918)
Come On In (with John Emerson, 1918)
Goodbye Bill (with John Emerson, 1918)
Hit-the-Trail Holiday (with John Emerson,
    based on the play by George M.
    Cohan, 1918)
Oh, You Women! (with John Emerson,
    1919)
Getting Mary Married (with John Emerson,
    1919)
A Temperamental Wife (with John
    Emerson, 1919)
A Virtuous Vamp (with John Emerson,
    based on a play by Clyde Fitch, 1919)
The Isle of Conquest (with John Emerson,
    based on the novel, "By Right of
    Conquest," by Arthur Hornblow,
    1919)
Two Weeks (with John Emerson, based on a
    play by Anthony Wharton, 1920)
In Search of a Sinner (with John Emerson,
    1920)
The Love Expert (with John Emerson,1920)
The Perfect Woman (with John Emerson,
    1920)
The Branded Woman (with John Emerson,
    based on the play by Oliver D. Bailey,
    1920)
Dangerous Business (with John Emerson,
    1921)
Mama's Affair (with John Emerson, based
    on the play by Rachel Barton Butler,
    1921)
A Woman's Place (with John Emerson,
    1921)

Red Hot Romance (with John Emerson,
    1922)
Polly of the Follies (with John Emerson,
    1922)
Dulcy (with John Emerson, based on the
    play by George S. Kaufman and Marc
    Connelly, 1923)
Three Miles Out (with John Emerson, based
    on a story by Neysa McMein, 1924)
Learning to Love (with John Emerson, 1925)
Publicity Madness (1927)
Gentlemen Prefer Blondes (with John
    Emerson, 1928)
The Struggle (1931)
Red-Headed Woman (based on the novel
    by Katharine Brush, 1932)
Blondie of the Follies (with Frances Marion,
    1932)
Hold Your Man (with Howard Emmett
    Rogers, 1933)
Midnight Mary (1933)
The Barbarian (with Elmer Harris, 1933)
Social Register (original story, 1934)
The Girl from Missouri (with John Emerson,
    1934)
Biography of a Bachelor Girl (based on a
    play by S.N. Behrman, 1934)
Riffraff (with Frances Marion and H.W.
    Haneman, 1935)
San Francisco (based on a story by Robert
    Hopkins, 1936)
Mama Steps Out (1937)
Saratoga (with Robert Hopkins, 1937)
The Great Canadian (1938)
Alaska (1938)
The Women (with Jane Murfin, based on
    the play by Clare Boothe, 1939)
Susan and God (based on the play by
    Rachel Crothers, 1940)
They Met in Bombay (with Edwin Justin
    Mayer and Leon Gordon, based on a
    story by Franz Kafka, 1941)
When Ladies Meet (with S.K. Lauren, based
    on a play by Rachel Crothers, 1941)
Blossoms in the Dust (based on a story by
    Ralph Wheelwright, 1941)
I Married an Angel (based on a musical by
    Vaszary Janos, Lorenz Hart and
    Richard Rodgers, 1942)
Gentlemen Prefer Blondes (original story,
    1953)

Index

Picture Credits